D1498672

Also by James Jespersen and Jane Fitz-Randolph

Time and Clocks for the Space Age

Mercury's Web

The Story of
Telecommunications

James Jespersen
and Jane Fitz-Randolph

Mercury's Web

The Story of
Telecommunications

ILLUSTRATED WITH

TECHNICAL DRAWINGS BY JUDITH FAST

AND PHOTOGRAPHS

Atheneum   1981   New York

LIBRARY OF CONGRESS CATALOGING IN PUBLICATION DATA

Jespersen, James.
Mercury's web.

SUMMARY: Discusses ways which information is processed
to be communicated over long distances.
1. Communication—Juvenile literature.
[1. Communication]   I. Fitz-Randolph, Jane.
II. Title.
P91.J4   001.51   81-2088
ISBN 0-689-30868-X   AACR2

Text copyright © 1981 by James Jespersen and Jane Fitz-Randolph
Illustrations copyright © 1981 by Atheneum Publishers, Inc.
Published simultaneously in Canada by
McClelland & Stewart, Ltd.
Type set by American—Stratford Graphic Services, Inc.
Brattleboro, Vermont
Manufactured by Fairfield Graphics, Fairfield,
Pennsylvania
Typography by M. M. Ahern
Layout by Marge Zaum
First Edition

To Lynn

Acknowledgments

The authors wish to thank Collier M. Smith for reading the manuscript and making many helpful suggestions.

NOTE TO READERS: You will find both meter and mile measurements in this book. We have used the measurement that was appropriate at the time.

Credits

Pictures were provided through the courtesy of the following:
American Telephone and Telegraph Company   178
Bell Laboratories   22, 165, 173, 199
Edison National Historic Site   72
Mount Wilson and Las Campanas Observatories, Carnegie Institution of Washington   210
National Astronomy and Ionosphere Center at Cornell University   217
National Captioning Institute   201
New York Public Library Picture Collection   26, 38, 41, 46, 53, 56, 58, 65, 70
United States Navy   19, 20

CONTENTS

Mercury's Web

The Story of Telecommunications

INTRODUCTION

In the southwestern corner of our continent there lives an unusual spider. Mexicans call him *mosquero,* the fly catcher. Unlike nearly all of the 50,000 or more identified species, this tiny spider lives in harmony with thousands of his kind in large communal webs. A fly that strays into the mosqueros' web becomes trapped in sticky strands of silk. Then signaled by the fly's buzzing wings, the spiders charge from the coves and crevices of their web, attacking first by dozens and then by tens of dozens. The fly quickly disappears in a swarming sheath of spiders.

Sometimes a honey bee blunders into a web; but the spiders, which are no match for honey bees, remain still. And when a fellow mosquero treads the web, his companions pay no attention. Most other kinds of spiders attack their own species as readily as they attack flies. Why is the mosquero so sociable?

The answer seems to be that his web is not only a home and a snare; it is also an intricate and delicate communication network that protects the spiders from attacking honey bees or each other. The silk strands have a curious property: they vibrate over only a small range of frequencies, from about 40 to 500 vibrations per second. The web hardly responds to a tuning fork touched against it unless the tuning fork vibrates within these frequencies.

Fly wings vibrate about 50 times per second; so a floundering fly trying to free itself from the web communicates its presence to the waiting spiders at once. But honey bee wings vibrate about 1000 times per second; so their beating produces barely a ripple in the web. And the much slower vibrations created by mosqueros moving across the web are not relayed by the silk strands.

Why has nature provided this method to protect mosqueros from honey bees and from each other? The mosquero, like most other spiders, has very poor vision. By the time he approaches a potential prey and comes close enough to identify it, it may be too late to save himself or his prey. Besides, there's a certain economy in letting the web reveal the presence of a fly. The spider doesn't have to patrol his net looking for trapped flies; he just sits at home "waiting for the phone to ring."

Man has his own web of communication. Some parts of the web are woven from strands of copper and glistening threads of translucent glass as fine as human hair. Other parts are invisible; these strands of communication are the radio waves that circle the earth and stretch to the very edge of the solar system—and even into interstellar space. Some scientists suspect that intelligent beings in other corners of the universe have spun their own webs of communication to bring their civilizations together—not physically, but mentally. On our own planet, Earthlings have built a giant antenna in Arecibo, Puerto Rico, that scans the sky seeking to catch in its mesh of aluminum plates some message fragment from a distant civilization in space.

This book is about communication. But it is also much more, for communication by itself is of little interest. There must be someone or something to interpret the communication, so that it leads to further understanding and perhaps some action. So this book is also about man's use of information and how he processes it to create new information—to his gain and sometimes to his loss. Information is both a resource and a challenge; we can use it to our advantage, or we can become smothered in it, like a hero returning to a New York ticker-tape parade.

Telecommunication, the use of electronic impulses to send, receive, distribute, process, and store information, is the fastest growing and most robust infant in the family of modern science and technology. So this book is not only about communication in general, but about telecommunication and how it developed.

I

The First Crude Strands

1.
The Gift of the Gods

One day—almost any day—you're cruising along on your bicycle and the traffic light at the intersection changes from orange to red. The car in front of you slows, then stops, its tail lights aglow. The right one blinks, and you brake to a stop behind the car.

Behind you, you hear a quick, light *toot-toot*. You look around, and your friend's dad waves. You smile and wave back.

A siren shrieks as a police car swings left around the corner and stops behind a pickup truck, which has also stopped just across the street. Stepping out of his car, the patrolman approaches the truck driver; he points to a sign at the intersection. On a white background the sign has a black arrow bent at a 45-degree angle to the left, with a red circle and slash-mark crossing out the arrow. The officer scowls; the truck driver looks disgusted.

Here in less than a minute you've seen, heard, and taken part in an amazing amount of communication, or exchange of information. It all seemed as natural and commonplace as breathing, and it did not include a single word. The traffic signal and the tail lights first warned you, then told you to stop. The blinking right tail light warned you not to pull up on that side because the car would turn right as soon as there was a break in traffic.

The short, friendly toot made you look around, and the exchange of waves and smiles said, "Hello, glad to see you." The siren told everyone to yield the right of way to an emergency vehicle. You recognized the policeman by his cap and his uniform, and the sign with the crossed-out left-turn arrow tells everyone what the truck driver did. The scowl and the look of disgust tell their own story.

Some of this communication is universal, and probably as old as mankind. Peoples of all cultures and in all parts of the world smile, wave, show their feelings by their facial expressions and body positions and movements. Even babies too young to talk will smile, laugh, "cloud up" and cry. Animals, too, show anger, frustration, pleasure. Horses and cats flatten their ears when angry. Dogs wag their tails in pleasure or greeting. Some dog and cat owners insist that their pets "smile."

Other signals in our little traffic drama are relatively new, but so familiar and widely used that they seem as much a part of nature as a smile or frown. Policemen have worn distinctive dress for generations, and the color red so commonly means "stop" that we could easily believe it had that association in prehistoric times. Yet there are still persons driving cars today who well remember when the only traffic signal was a policeman with a shrill whistle and waving arms, and when a driver's stop and turn signals were his own left arm stuck out the car window in a certain position.

Besides all this *nonverbal* communication that you saw and heard at the intersection, there were also several other kinds of messages, or signals. A bumper sticker on the car ahead, the seal or "logo" on the police car, the license plates on the various cars and perhaps your bicycle are all sources of information. Each car has a label and certain design features that show its make and model.

Perhaps you yourself were wearing a tee-shirt with a picture or words or both, or a sweater that tells by its colors

where you go to school. As you rode along, maybe you were
listening to a favorite song on your transistor radio. And you
glanced at your watch to see if you'd be home in time to
catch the ball game on TV. Possibly you were on your way
to the library to exchange some books, or to write part of
your science report; you might use the machine there to
make a photocopy of a chart you want to include. And probably you'll type the final copy of your paper.

These are only a few of the scores of *media* in the vast
communication web that we all live in every day—those we
can easily see and hear. There are others surrounding us
every moment of the day and night. Some messages travel
specifically from sender to receiver on metal wires or fibers
of glass. Others ripple out through the air in all directions
from radio and television transmitters. They may travel to a
satellite in outer space and back to millions of receivers on
the earth in less than a second. Or they may creep along the
ground and across the oceans, following the curvature of the
earth's surface. They may be in the form of codes, rushing
back and forth between computers.

It's been said that no creature on earth is less conscious
of water than a fish. Immersed in water as it is, and never
having known any other kind of environment, it could not—
if it were a reasoning creature—imagine anything else. And
it would have a hard time describing what water is like because it has never stood off and looked at water from the
outside. Caught up in and surrounded as we are by an intricate web of many kinds of communication systems, it's hard
for us to imagine a world not only without television, telephones, and radios, but without books and magazines and
newspapers, or even writing. Unless we stop to think about
it, we don't realize that all our cameras, microscopes, bath-
room scales, thermometers, and hundreds of other everyday
devices are simply instruments for extracting, transferring,
and storing information.

Like the tail lights that glow when a driver puts his foot on the brake, most of today's communication is automated; and computers do far more "talking" to each other than people do. *Information* today is more than 50 percent of the gross national product in the United States. When we realize that this is more than all the food we eat, the clothes we wear, the houses we live in, and the cars we drive all added together, we begin to see just how big and important the information and communication industries are, and what a large part they play in shaping the way we live.

If it's hard to think of a world without the modern instruments we take for granted, it's even harder to imagine a world without language. No one knows when and where, or even how language first appeared. There are no bones or pottery shards or other artifacts from which to reconstruct ancient languages. But scientists generally agree that there were no human beings anywhere without a language, and that no other creatures have a true language. Cows moo and dogs bark, but the sounds are the same as those they've been making since they first existed and in all parts of the world. No animals can talk about something that is not present where they are, or about abstract ideas like beauty or justice. The people of early civilizations thought language so mysterious and wonderful that they considered it a special gift from the gods; the Romans attributed it to Mercury, the messenger of the gods.

It's reasonable to speculate that "body language" along with various simple sounds must have existed as long as man himself. The very first human beings probably laughed, cried, shouted, moaned. Doubtless they made loud and soft sounds, high-pitched and low-pitched ones. They may easily have motioned to one another to come or to follow and have stamped a foot in anger.

But this kind of communication was limited to what was at hand. Two individuals could not discuss the birds they saw yesterday or the fish they hoped to catch tomorrow. They needed *symbols,* words that would stand for or mean "bird" and "fish," "yesterday" and "tomorrow." That is, they needed a *language.* Language is the first essential for communication, whether it's a language spoken or written by a certain group of people, the language of music expressed as notes of different pitches or symbols drawn on a staff, or digital "bits" rushing through copper wires to a "memory bank"—electronic language.

The basic elements of all languages—and all kinds of languages—are the same, and all are governed by the laws of nature. One of the first and most obvious requirements is for a *sender* and a *receiver,* and for agreement between sender and receiver as to what the various symbols of their language mean. If the sender makes a sound that means "fish" to him, but that means "bird" or "dog"—or maybe nothing at all— to the receiver, their communication will quickly break down. Furthermore, these symbols must be different enough from each other so that they cannot be easily confused; this is especially important for pairs of words like *black* and *white,* or *left* and *right.* It would not be good to have the symbols for *yes* and *no* sound or look very much alike.

Another necessity for any language is some sort of grammar, or rules that show relationships of the different symbols or words. *The boy killed the shark* uses the same words as *The shark killed the boy,* but the grammar—in this case the order of the words—makes the meaning quite different. Similarly, sender and receiver need to be able to distinguish between a single warrior and a whole band of warriors, and between *I went* and *I will go.*

Then there's the question of what *medium* the language is to use. Among the earliest peoples, the only medium was the sound waves that carried the sender's speech or shouts, or the light waves that made it possible for the receiver to see his waving arms. Today we have all sorts of media—books, magazines, newspapers, letters, and other print media; pictures, films, and magnetic tapes; wires and glass fibers; radio and television waves.

No language is perfect, and none can serve all purposes equally well. No medium is ideal or even suitable for all situations. A sender may wish to *broadcast* his message to as many receivers as possible, or he may wish to *narrowcast* to a very specific audience—just one person perhaps. The audience may be a special kind of receivers, such as deaf or blind persons. The greatest need may be to get the message through in a hurry, or to send it across a great distance, or to protect it from reaching an enemy. So depending on the purposes and needs, the sender chooses or invents a language and medium that seem to serve him best.

Throughout history people have tried very hard to make their messages travel farther, faster, and more securely with the least possible error and distortion. Today, as our electronic communication systems multiply and grow ever more complex and sophisticated, processing information becomes more and more challenging. As we shall see, the same laws of nature that governed the earliest communication still apply to these modern systems. One of these laws seems to be that we can't have everything; invariably we have to settle for some sort of trade-off. Voice radio signals between ships at sea are fairly simple, but they can be picked up by other, possibly enemy ships; flag signals make no sound, but they can travel over only a limited distance and are useless in a fog or at night. If the gods gave language to mankind, they put some restrictions on their gift and have left us with some hard choices and difficult problems to work out.

2.
Smoke Signals & Silicon Chips

It was the summer of 1588. A fleet of 132 Spanish ships manned by 8,000 sailors and 19,000 marines advanced in a crescent formation into the English Channel. The English mainland was soon alive with fire beacons and columns of smoke that passed the word that the Spanish were attacking. Within 20 minutes the message had traveled 200 miles, from Plymouth to London. Alerted by the signals, English seamen swarmed into their ships and began the campaign that defeated the Spanish Armada and ended Spain's position as a sea power in the world.

Nearly two centuries later, and on the other side of the Atlantic Ocean, the English military forces were themselves the target of another signal scheme. Visitors to Boston today are shown the spot where Paul Revere waited on his horse on the night of his famous ride, watching for the lantern signal from the belfry of Old North Church. A fellow patriot in the high church tower would hang a lantern signal—"one if by land, two if by sea"—so that Revere could dash to Lexington and tell the undermanned American troops where and how the British were about to attack.

This message is a little more complex than the one relayed by the smoke signals. The lantern signal contained *two* possible messages: one lantern meant that attackers were coming by land, and two meant they were coming by sea. Today the message would have to be even more complicated: by land, by sea, or by air. If we wished to extend Paul Revere's scheme to fit today's situation, we would need three lanterns.

But then it might occur to someone that *one* lantern is enough: One *flash* means by land, two flashes mean by sea, and three flashes mean by air. And in case the invasion was proceeding on all three fronts, four flashes could mean by land, sea, *and* air.

As the message from the church steeple gets more complicated, another problem arises: The man on the horse may not remember what the flashes mean. Was one flash "by sea" or "by air"? Or what if it's foggy, and the watcher isn't sure whether he saw two flashes or three? Or what if the fog is so dense that he can't see *any* flashes?

In that case there must be some other, backup plan. One clang of the Old North Church bell means by land; two mean by sea, and so on. But then a clanging church bell in the middle of the night might arouse people who were better left asleep.

In a small way, we have just described the kinds of problems that face the designers and operators of today's communication and information systems. What is the best kind of signal to insure that the message will reach the intended receiver? How can we code the message to keep "the enemy" from reading its meaning? How do we make sure that the receiver knows what the various symbols mean? What if several persons want to send messages at the same time and we have only one "lantern"? If we want to send huge quantities of information, how can we store it at the receiving end?

As we've said, no communication system is perfect, and solving one problem often creates new ones. People have made good use of the knowledge and materials they had to develop communication devices to meet their needs. Sometimes, as in the two examples we've just seen, their ingenuity made the difference between a nation's defeat or victory. Not all communication needs, fortunately, are so crucial or dramatic. Swiss and Austrian mountain dwellers developed a peculiar, far-reaching cry or *yodel* that carried from peak to peak across deep gorges. People of many cultures blew on horns or trumpets, different combinations of notes meaning different things. At first the trumpets were actual animal horns or sea shells. Later they were made of brass or silver. Bugles and bugle calls still serve as good signals in some military groups and other organizations such as summer camps.

Visitors to Africa have told fascinating stories of the "talking drums" made by the natives. By varying the pitch and tempo of the beats, the drummer can imitate the native speech, sending simple messages quite "readably." The message may travel ten miles or so, and then be relayed by another drummer, so that it can cover 200 miles or more almost as quickly as a telegram could travel.

To make sure the message gets through, the drummer repeats it over and over. As we shall see, repeating messages is an important part of modern communication systems. Each village—and often each family—has its own code or "telephone number," so that messages can be quite specific. But of course there's no chance for privacy. If the message says, "John, come home and clean your hut," everyone within earshot of the drum knows John's sloppy habits.

This is also a disadvantage with all "line of sight" methods of communication. The North American Plains Indians used smoke signals to send messages—something that wouldn't work at all in dense African jungles where one cannot see out. They had codes that used smoke columns from two or more fires to mean different things; a more sophisticated system involved covering and uncovering the fire with a blanket, so that separate puffs of smoke rose skyward. But there was no way to send a smoke signal to just a chosen receiver, or to keep the sender's location secret. And weather conditions, even darkness, closed down the system much of the time. At best the signal could be seen only 20 to 30 miles away, and of course it can't travel through obstructions or around corners. As we shall see later, our modern electronic systems have to be designed to cope with these same kinds of limitations.

The American Indians also developed a remarkable language that anthropologists say was their greatest achievement. Their *sign language* made it possible for some 30 tribes that couldn't understand one another's spoken language to communicate with each other and with white men who learned the language. It was a complex system, so well developed that individuals could "talk" about abstract ideas as well as objects. Some Boy Scouts of different countries and also men who belong to Rotary International learn Indian sign language so that they can communicate with one another at international meetings.

Many deaf persons "sign" to communicate with one another and with others who learn the language. American Sign Language (Ameslan) is today the third most widely used language in the United States. Sign language, too, has its advantages and limitations. It is absolutely silent, and two or several persons can discuss something without even a whisper alerting others to their presence; two hunters some distance apart can plan their attack on an unsuspecting quarry. But the participants must be fairly close to each other —unless the sender is on television—and sign language is useless in the dark.

Another kind of sign language, with a much longer although limited range, uses flags for a medium. Communication between ships has always been a necessity and a challenge. So it's not surprising that the world's fleets and navies have developed ingenious schemes to meet the challenge. Before the invention of electronic communication, they had developed flag codes, which are still vital to naval operations. Although today's ships have highly sophisticated electronic navigation and communication systems, there are often situations in which, for security reasons, these systems cannot be used. So in addition to mastering the Morse code of dots and dashes, signalmen must also be able to send and receive flag-hoist and semaphore messages.

The flaghoist system uses flags of different shapes and color combinations for each letter and numeral, plus a number of other pennants that mean "emergency," "turn," "star-board," and so on. The signalman spells out his message by attaching the flags to a rope or halyard and hoisting the display to a yardarm so that it can be read by the signalmen on the other ship or ships.

Flaghoist signal

Semaphore signaling uses two hand-held flags. The sender spells out the message word by word, the positions of his arms indicating each letter. These flag systems may seem cumbersome in this day of electronics, but they are effective, and they travel much faster than a personal messenger could go because the signal itself travels at the speed of light.

Railroads adapted the semaphore idea to their own

Semaphore alphabet and special signals

needs, to send messages to engineers and crews of trains moving into or out of railroad yards or stations. At first the mechanical devices were operated manually; today they are operated electronically from a console in a control room.

Perhaps by now we're beginning to see how cleverly different people with different needs tie themselves together with different kinds of communication lines. The strands crisscross and touch, sometimes strengthening each other, sometimes duplicating or even interfering with each other, in a web that's growing more and more complex. In today's society, the amount of information that flows through the web every second of the day and night would quickly swamp even the sum total of all human minds. Only computers have the capacity to collect, sort, send, receive, store, and digest this flood of information—and misinformation and "garbage."

The most visible parts of today's information and communication systems are common household items. We're quite at ease with telephones, radios, television sets, stereos, tape recorders, and hand-held calculators. Some 300,000 American homes have microcomputers, and the number is growing rapidly. We can buy devices that let us play games on our TV sets, and there are chess-playing machines, held easily in one's hands, that challenge even the master chess players. Our microwave ovens know when the roast is done, and some electronic watches not only tell us the time but do calculations and even remember telephone numbers that we use most often.

Many of the elements of communication systems are less visible. A few years ago a telephone call was "put through" manually by an operator sitting at a switchboard. Today most of these manual operations have been replaced by electronic devices, many of which are under computer control. The number of operations completed each day by these automatic systems is so great that if every man, woman, and child in the United States all worked as telephone operators, we could not duplicate them. Air traffic controllers at busy airports use computers and radar to keep track of aircraft arriving and departing by the minute on a maze of interconnected runways; passenger reservations for scores of different airlines departing from hundreds of different airports are made almost instantly at any one of hundreds of locations.

The device that has made all of these and hundreds of other developments possible is about the size of your little fingernail; and it is made almost entirely of silicon, the main component of sand and one of the most abundant elements on the surface of the earth. This tiny device, called a *chip*,

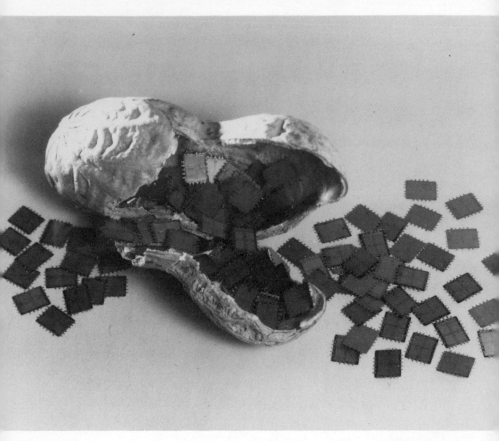

*A peanut shell
can hold
180 electronic chips*

has replaced the bulky, unreliable vacuum tubes and mazes of wires that were themselves once considered marvels in early television sets: it has the computing power of the huge, room-size computer of 30 years ago. Probably the chip will continue to change our lives and societies in ways that will surpass the changes brought about by the Industrial Revolution in the early 1900s. But unlike the steam engine and the whirring and clanging machines of the Industrial Revolution, the chip operates silently, uses very little energy, practically never wears out, and is very cheap. We will learn much more about chips later.

Still, the capabilities of our electronic devices are limited by the same laws of nature that govern drum beats and flag signals. The fire beacons used by the English in 1588 relayed their message at speeds that have not been surpassed today. According to our present understanding of nature, no signal can travel faster than the speed of light. This limit affects the speed of computers, and even our ability to communicate with distant parts of the universe where societies of intelligent beings may live.

Since the jostling packets of information in computers cannot travel faster than the speed of light, the "biggest" computers are becoming smaller and smaller, so that the information packets can make their journey in the least time possible. But we cannot compress the universe; and some parts of the universe are so distant that if signals had been launched from them even millions of years ago, they would not yet have reached the earth. By the same principle, programs from our own early days of television are now expanding away from the earth in spherical shells which, by this time, have just passed a few dozen of our nearest stars. In spite of these difficulties, though, scientists have directed huge antennas toward the heavens with the slim hope that some message will one day be detected. We shall discuss these efforts later, but first we must understand more about early communication schemes—specifically, writing.

3.
From Pictographs to ABC

You've just spent your all for a fielders mitt, and you're not going to take any chances that someone else may claim it. So you print your name boldly with black, waterproof ink where it cannot be hidden or mistaken. Simple. You've been identifying your books, sweaters, sports equipment, and other possessions this way for years. Probably the first thing you learned to write or print was your name.

What you did was much like what archaeologists believe was the very earliest "writing." Primitive peoples needed to mark their belongings as their own—a favorite tool or weapon made of bone or stone perhaps. They did not print their names, for there were no letters. So they made up a symbol, often a simple drawing of an animal or bird, that they and everyone else recognized as their own individual mark.

Early peoples also wanted to record their activities. Pictures scratched or carved on the walls of caves deep underground in France and Spain are known to be at least 15 to 25 thousand years old. Pictures on other stone surfaces in various parts of the world have preserved accounts of animal hunts, battles, adventures, and events.

Such communication has obvious limitations. To "read"

the pictures, one must go to where the pictures are, and the pictures can tell only part of the story, although it's amazing how much. But to get the details, there had to be an interpreter—the artist himself, or perhaps someone who had listened to the story as the artist made the picture. Probably it was much the same as when you show a friend some snapshots you've made and you explain, "This was on our camping trip, and you can see the raccoon there in the tree where my dog chased it."

Little by little, the *pictographs* that symbolized such things as the sun, a river, and so on became so familiar that the artist could simplify them. Just the head of an ox was enough to indicate the whole animal, and a human foot could represent walking or going somewhere. Even abstract ideas such as sorrow could be shown by a human eye with tears dripping from it.

But this was still a long way from actual writing. A big breakthrough came when someone—or probably several some-ones—got the idea of using the symbols to mean both the thing pictured and the *sound* of its name. The sound of a word had never been associated with its picture before. You've doubtless enjoyed a variation of this idea in working out *rebus* puzzles, which might say something like "I (saw) him (duck) behind the (chair man) in the (pan tree)."

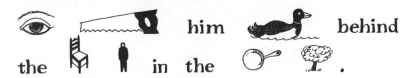

The big difference is that this sentence has some pictures and some words—and that's a very big difference, since there's no satisfactory way to express the words in pictures.

True writing came with a system that represented the sounds of each *syllable* in the language. It was invented some 5,000 years ago by people known as Sumerians who lived in what is today Iraq. The symbols were made up of triangles and short, straight lines; scholars who studied them called the writing *cuneiform,* meaning "wedge-shaped." The symbols were drawn on a pad or tablet of wet clay with a stylus or pen made by cutting a reed diagonally.

During the next two or three thousand years cuneiform writing spread to other countries with different languages. Since there are a great many different possible syllables in any language, learning the thousands of symbols in the *syllabary* was a very large undertaking. Few persons—only priests and lawyers at first—had the leisure time to learn to read and write. Later, young men who became *scribes* earned a good income in a highly respected occupation. Most of the culture, learning, and commerce centered around the temples, and people believed that once again the gods had favored lowly human beings, this time with the marvelous gift of writing.

Still the mortals who worked with the reeds and wet clay had some of the same problems as mortals who use computers for their communication systems today. One was the *form* the writing should take, and we find a lot of experimentation among the scribes. At first they wrote their symbols in columns, beginning in the upper right-hand corner of the tablet and moving from top to bottom and from right to left.

A sample of cuneiform writing on a clay tablet

Then to keep from messing up what they'd just written, some scribes turned the tablet sidewise and worked across its surface. Some worked clear around the outer edge of the tablet and then moved inward toward the middle. Some worked with alternating lines, the first moving from right to left and the next from left to right. Eventually they settled for left to right and top to bottom, just as we write.

Another problem, which is even more troublesome in present-day electronic communication, was how to protect the message from change or forgery. It was like writing an important document with a pencil, which could be easily erased, for the clay could be moistened and the writing changed. The Sumerians solved the problem by baking the tablets in ovens, much as we fire pottery today.

Anthropologists believe that true writing was invented only three times at most in the whole history of the world. Long after the Sumerians' cuneiform writing had spread around the Persian Gulf, a similar system of syllable symbols appeared in China, where it is still used today. No one is sure whether it was invented there or imported from the Persian Gulf. Still later the Mayan Indians of the Western Hemisphere invented their own writing.

More people speak Chinese today than any other language. Only half as many speak English, the second most common language. Since the Chinese still use their original writing system, and since it illustrates so well some of the advantages and problems of communication that we still have today, we'll discuss it a little further. The Chinese wrote on silk, bamboo, and wood or bark, and they used a brush and ink instead of a stylus. Paper was invented in China in the first century A.D., and some of the earliest scrolls contain beautiful handwriting or *calligraphy*.

One big advantage of the Chinese writing is that scholars today can read the ancient manuscripts almost as easily as they can the current writings. The written language does not change, even though the spoken language has changed greatly and broken into many dialects; people who speak one dialect are often unable to understand those who speak another, but those who know how to read can all read a common language.

Still, the disadvantages of this language of "syllable pictures" are enormous—especially when it comes to trying to cope with electronic communication. There are some 40,000 different symbols in the Chinese syllabary. This collection has been simplified to less than half that many for everyday business use. But even this, compared to the 26 letters of our

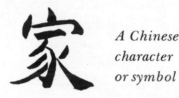

A Chinese character or symbol

English alphabet, is staggering.

There are very few sounds in the Chinese language, and nearly all words have just one syllable. This means that each sound or word must have many different meanings. The one word *i*, for example, has more than 60 different meanings. The way a speaker and listener know which one is meant is by the sense it makes and the way it's *said*. It may start at one pitch and then rise to mean one thing, or fall to mean another; Chinese is a *tonal* language.

These characteristics made it seem at first that it was impossible to send a telegram in Chinese. There's no way to send the symbols, and phonetic spelling of the spoken words would be too confusing. The problem was finally solved by making a code that assigns numbers from 0001 to 9999 to the 10,000 characters most often used.

This scheme doesn't work so well, however, with other

kinds of electronic communication. Over the past 30 years of television, the only real improvement has been the introduction of color. But we are now in the midst of a new development called "teletext." With present TV technology, viewers have to look at a program when it is on—unless they have a video tape recorder. With teletext a viewer can get certain kinds of "written" information such as weather forecasts or sports scores whenever he wishes.

In countries where the written language uses only 20 or 30 symbols in an alphabet similar to our own, teletext is fairly easy to implement. But in countries like China or Japan the situation is much more complicated because the teletext part of a TV set must be able to display several thousand complex symbols.

Breaking down syllables into *letters* that would indicate certain sounds was a stroke of pure genius. Language scientists say that the alphabet was invented only once in the whole history of mankind, and they believe it could have been invented by a single individual. It first appeared in Palestine in the 17th or 18th century B.C., among people known as Canaanites. This first alphabet made it possible to express all the sounds of the language with just 22 symbols, or letters, instead of thousands of complex signs. All other alphabets in the world grew from this one. Our own grew out of the one that the Greeks adapted and improved, which they got from the Persians.

At first, all of the letters were capitals, and no space was left between the words. Neither was there any punctuation. This was the general practice until about the 10th century A.D.:

ARENTYOUGLADYOUDONTHAVETOREADLIKETHIS

The alphabet made writing and reading much easier, so many more people learned how. But there was little to read except family records, laws and decrees, and tax receipts. Each book and scroll had to be written or printed by hand. The next big breakthrough was the invention of movable type in the fifteenth century. Paper making advanced, and within 50 years after Johann Gutenberg invented the printing press in 1454, there were nearly 10 million books in existence.

When craftsmen began making several or many copies of the same book, there was a much greater need to do it right. Words that had been spelled in different ways by different writers had to be standardized. Grammar and "style" became much more important. The written or printed language became the authentic language.

By the time American boys and girls reach junior high school, they've discovered that the English language has many peculiarities that make it far from perfect. The grammar is sometimes confusing, and the spelling frequently makes no sense at all. Often there's no way to tell from the way a word is said how it should be spelled, or from the way it's spelled how it is pronounced. Still, in spite of its contradictions and limitations, our alphabet serves us very well. And fortunately, it's not too difficult to translate it into "electronic language," as we shall see.

The brief tour we've had through the world's communication web in these first three chapters has given us some idea of the way the web was formed. We might say that these first crude strands "just happened" as human beings reached out to their fellow human beings. The systems we shall look at in Section II resulted largely from random experiments with unfolding knowledge of electricity and magnetism. And the systems we shall explore in Section III were developed very specifically by skilled scientists working with the most recent concepts of physics and the laws of nature, and the most advanced technologies. Each new strand of the complex web brings new challenges and new possibilities.

II

Wires and Wireless

4.
Dots & Dashes

As reading, writing, and printing became common, people kept better records of events and the records had a better chance of survival. Few names of individuals are associated with inventions and developments before the printing press. Certainly no one knows who first blew notes on a cow's horn or carved out a drum that could talk. We have no record of who suggested cuneiform writing or what individual invented the alphabet. Certainly he must have ranked as an Edison or an Einstein among his people. Later, there were, and still are, doubts about the authorship of some of Shakespeare's writings in the sixteenth century.

But by the time electricity began to play a part in communication technology in the early 1800s, there were reliable records of people's activities. Scientists often published accounts of their work for other scientists to read; and as the idea of copyrights and patents of original works grew, inventors and scientists found it important to keep records of their work.

So we suddenly begin to meet many individuals who played a part in weaving the world's communication web. Some will be familiar to you, and some probably unknown.

Today nearly everyone knows that electricity and magnetism are related. Beginning science books explain how electricity is generated by coils of copper wire spinning between the poles of giant magnets. Probably you have done simple experiments that show how ordinary needles become magnetized when they are placed near loops of wire carrying electric currents. The picture tube in your TV set is just one of hundreds of modern inventions based on the principle of the relationship between electricity and magnetism.

In the early 1800s, however, no one understood this relationship—or realized that there was such a connection. Magnetism was well known to early navigators, whose magnetized compass needles pointed toward the earth's north pole. And ancient peoples had discovered the mysterious magnetic properties of certain kinds of metallike rocks called lodestones.

People knew about Benjamin Franklin's experiments with lightning in the mid-1700s, and they were quite familiar with the electricity that crackled around their ears when they combed their hair with a hard-rubber comb. But how was this electricity related to the current that flowed from the first battery invented in 1800?

In those days "electricity" meant *static* electricity—the kind generated by the comb in your hair and that leaps from your finger toward some unsuspecting victim after you've shuffled your feet across a rug. It's the troublesome electricity that makes it necessary to spray your records and your clothes tumbled in the drier with antistatic preparations—especially in very dry climates.

Galvanism was the term that referred to the electric currents generated by batteries; it was named for Luigi Galvani, an Italian physiologist whose chance discovery of the reaction of a frog's leg to metallic conductors led to the development of the battery.

But during the winter of 1820, a Danish physicist, Hans Christian Øersted, performed an experiment that changed scientists' concepts of electricity. Øersted was lecturing to a class of students on the subject of magnetism, electricity, and galvanism. He had a hunch that there might be some connection between electricity and magnetism, but he had no clear idea of how to go about examining his hunch. As a test, he placed a wire carrying a galvanic current above and at right angles to a compass needle. Nothing happened. But after class he tried his experiment again. This time he lined up the wire and the needle in the same direction. Instantly the needle twisted to the side; and when he reversed the current by switching the wires at the battery terminals, the needle twisted in the other direction, as shown in Figure 1.

This was a very peculiar result. In the past, experience had always indicated that the "force" between two objects acted along a line connecting the two objects. For example, a rock dropped from a tall building falls toward the center of the earth, and not in some sideways direction. Similarly, the north and south poles of two bar magnets, held near each other, attract each other along a line running from the north pole of one magnet to the south pole of the other. But Øersted's result seemed to violate this rule. When he aligned the needle with the direction of the current, the needle swung at right angles to the direction of the current.

Further experiments revealed why Øersted obtained this

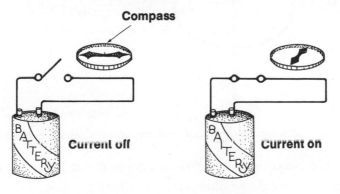

fig. 1   *Øersted's Discovery*

strange result. The current running through the wire sets up a *magnetic force,* but the direction of this force is not along the direction of the wire, as we might expect; instead, it runs in concentric circles around the wire, as shown in Figure 2. So when a magnet—such as a compass needle—is brought near the current-carrying wire, the magnet lines up with the direction of the magnetic lines of force created by the current; and these are at right angles to the wire.

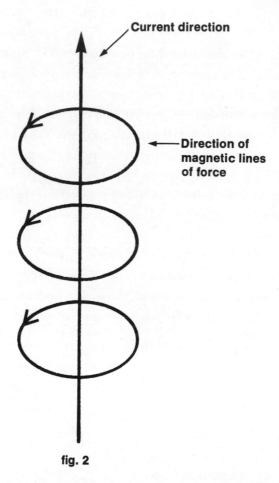

Current direction

Direction of
magnetic lines
of force

fig. 2

We can summarize Øersted's experiments by saying that "electric currents produce magnetic lines of force that circle the current-carrying wire or conductor." This, we shall see later, turned out to be the first of four general laws that describe the behavior of electricity and magnetism. Øersted first published the results of his experiments in Latin. Then on July 21, 1820, his works appeared at the same time in two French scientific publications, this time in French.

A French mathematics professor, André-Marie Ampère, repeated Øersted's experiments, as well as some new ones of his own. Within two months he had established what today we call the science of *electrodynamics*. Ampère had incorporated Øersted's results into a more complete theory that explained a great many magnetic phenomena, including the earth's magnetism, in terms of electric currents.

Ampère was interested mainly in the basic laws that govern electricity. But he also had a practical side that led him to realize that his work provided a basis for what we would now recognize as a primitive form of the telegraph. He imagined a system of wires connecting the sender and receiver, with a wire for each letter of the alphabet. To spell out the words of his message, the sender would send a current down the wire that corresponded to the letter he wished to transmit. Each of the wires at the receiver's end passed near a magnetized needle that indicated the same letter as the one sent. So as the sender sent his currents down the appropriate wires, the letters moved in step to the receiver's end, spelling out the message.

It was another 20 years—1833—before such an electromagnetic telegraph was actually built, in Germany. Instead of the many-wired system that Ampère imagined, the German system had just two wires stretched from rooftop to rooftop, spanning a distance of 2.3 kilometers. To get around the problem of providing a wire for each letter of the alphabet by using coded transmissions, various sequences of currents were sent down the "line" wire to represent the different letters.

At the receiving end, a compasslike device with a tiny

André Marie Ampère
invented an early
telegraph system
that was very
complicated.

mirror attached to the magnetized needle detected the currents. The mirror magnified the very small movements of the needle, in much the same way that you have doubtless flashed a reflected spot of sunlight all around a room by tilting a mirror in your hand just very slightly. A small telescope a few feet away, pointed at the mirror, could detect the mirror's tiny movements. Cumbersome as their device seems, a variation of it played an important role in the operation of the first successful transatlantic cable, as we shall see.

Others also realized that the principles of electro-dynamics pointed the way to telegraphy. In England a 6-wire, 5-needle telegraph system was introduced and patented in 1838. The five needles were mounted on a board containing the letters of the alphabet and the numbers 0 through 9. The letters and numbers were arranged so that deflections of any two needles pointed to a particular number or letter, as shown in Figure 3.

Needles 2 and 5
point to the letter F

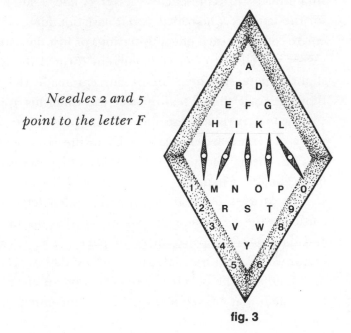

fig. 3

Although this system thrived in England, it was the system developed by an American portrait painter, Samuel F. B. Morse, that dominated the telegraph system in America and continental Europe. Morse, who also had an interest in invention and science, first sketched out his ideas in 1832. To save costs by having as few wires as possible, he planned to use a coded transmission similar to the German system. Part of the genius of the Morse telegraph plan was the scheme he developed for coding the letters and numbers. Morse and a friend visited the typesetting room of a local newspaper. The typesetter showed them how he needed more of certain letters than others. Morse and his friend systematically went through the typesetter's trays to find out which letters he used most. They discovered that *e* and *t* were the most used letters; and as you might expect, *x* was needed least often.

Morse reasoned that the shortest code symbols should be chosen for the most-used letters, and the longer symbols should stand for the letters used least often. So he chose a single dot   to represent the letter *e,* and a single dash for the letter *t; x* he coded as dot-dash-dot-dot-   . His entire code consisted of combinations of just dots and dashes; a very short burst of electric current formed the dot, and a slightly more sustained bit of current made the dash. Although Morse didn't realize it at the time, his approach to coding that involved the idea of the probability of occurrence of certain letters was crucial to the later development of the "theory of communication," which we shall learn more about in Chapter 17.

In Morse's original system, the coded letters were recorded at the receiving end by a pencil that marked the dots and dashes on a moving piece of paper. The telegraph operator would then translate the dots and dashes on the paper into English. The pencil was operated by an electromechanical system that clicked along with the incoming signal; and

Samuel F. B. Morse
was the father
of the Morse code
of dots and dashes.

the operators soon realized that by listening to the clicks they could translate and write down the message directly, and that the pencil device was unnecessary.

One of Morse's partners, who was more mechanically inclined than Morse, made many important additions, including the invention of the telegraph key. Other people also contributed to the system. The man who erected Morse's first telegraph line used glass doorknobs as insulators on the arms of telegraph poles; and Joseph Henry, one of America's most famous early scientists, helped Morse develop a system to relay messages from one telegraph company to another.

In 1843, the United States Congress gave Morse $30,000 to install a line about 40 miles long connecting Washington, D.C., to Baltimore, Maryland. The first words sent over the line, on May 24, 1844, were the now well-known message, "What hath God wrought?"

By 1860, telegraph lines linked most of the major cities of the United States, especially in the populous northeast. The wires were strung on poles beside the railroads, which were also in a period of great growth. Each contributed to the extension of the other, as the telegraph became vital to the railroads for keeping track of their trains, sending messages about storms and damaged tracks, and so on. The well-developed system of railroads and telegraph lines in the northern states gave the Union forces an enormous advantage over the South during the Civil War. And the Pacific Telegraph line that replaced the Pony Express across the Great Plains in 1862 cut communication time from a minimum of two weeks to send a message and receive a reply, to just minutes. Without the telegraph, building the Union Pacific Railroad would have been next to impossible.

The early telegraph system in the United States, however, was composed of many small companies. This posed a problem for sending long-distance telegrams, for they had to be retransmitted from company to company. Starting about 1856, many of the small companies were consolidated into what became the Western Union Telegraph Company by 1866. It consisted of more than 2,500 stations.

Marvelous as the telegraph was, the lines came to a halt when they reached the sea. As early as 1842, Morse had laid short lines in New York Harbor, but as we shall learn in the next chapter, this was child's play compared with laying a cable across the Atlantic Ocean.

5.
Queen Victoria's Message

The early telegraph wires that crisscrossed the United States were largely bare, often made of iron. They were not at all suitable for service in the salty, corrosive, electricity-conducting waters of the oceans. Morse's first submarine cable in New York Harbor was of copper wire insulated in part with India rubber, but the insulation soon failed. Insulation that was dissolved by salt water, penetrated by sea borers and other creatures, or cut and torn by rocks on the ocean floor became an old story before the art of manufacturing submarine cables was perfected.

By 1848 many insulating materials had been tested and found unsuitable. Manufacturers tried cotton treated with various chemicals, tarred rope, split rattan, and India rubber. The material that showed the greatest promise was gutta-percha, a gum-like substance made from the sap of a Malayan tree.

In the late summer of 1850, a single strand of copper wire coated with gutta-percha was laid between Dover, England, and Calais, France. Even though the cable failed, its promoters were sure they were on the right track; so they laid another cable the next year. This one was in use for nearly 25 years before it failed; and for 70 years after its introduction, gutta-percha remained the best known material for insulating submarine cables.

The first attempt to connect America and Europe by a submarine cable crossing the Atlantic Ocean was made in 1857. But techniques for laying the thousands of miles of cable, sometimes at a depth of more than 2,000 fathoms, had not been perfected. The cable broke in very deep water and could not be recovered. Two more attempts were made the following year, and the second of these operated successfully for about one month.

There was great excitement on both sides of the Atlantic, and Queen Victoria of England sent a 90-word message to United States President James Buchanan that read in part: "The Queen wishes to congratulate the President on the successful completion of the great international work, in which the Queen has taken great interest."

Cyrus W. Field, an American financier who had steadfastly supported the project, became an international hero. But when the cable failed on September 1, Field went from hero to international villain almost overnight. He was accused of bilking the public, and some people even speculated that no cable had been laid—that the purported message from Queen Victoria was a hoax.

There were also other problems, of a scientific nature; Lord Kelvin, a famous English scientist who had been associated with Field in backing the cable projects, was a key figure in solving these. Lord Kelvin's father was a mathematics teacher and textbook writer. He taught his young son most of the mathematics known at that time, and by age ten he had entered the University of Glasgow, in Scotland. His first two scientific papers were published by the time he was 17. They were a defense of some work done by a French mathematician who had developed some powerful mathematical tools for studying the flow of heat through various objects.

Lord Kelvin realized that the French mathematician's methods could be applied to the flow of electricity through

*Lord Kelvin designed
the first practical
transatlantic cable.*

a cable. On the basis of this work—and enthusiastic support from his father—he was named professor of natural philosophy at Glasgow at the age of 22. He went on to do basic work in many different scientific areas, including the absolute temperature scale; the unit of this scale, the Kelvin, is named after him. But it is his inventions and theoretical work on submarine cables that interest us here.

In the excitement of the successful transmission of the first trans-Atlantic message, it was little noted that Queen Victoria's 90-word message had required 16 hours to transmit, even though the cable was continuous and well-insulated from the sea. The source of the problem was what at that time was called "retardation of the signal."

A friend of Lord Kelvin's had written him a letter in 1854, four years before Queen Victoria's message, inquiring about the retardation problem, which had been noticed in a shorter cable connecting England and the Netherlands. The problem was that although it took only an instant to "key in" a dot or a dash at the transmission end of the cable, it took almost a tenth of a second for the current in the cable to build up to its maximum strength at the receiving end. This limited the signaling rate to about five dots or dashes per second.

Lord Kelvin used his adaptation of the French mathematician's method to analyze the problem, and he concluded that the problem grew worse as the length of the cable increased. He calculated that the retardation for a cable crossing the Atlantic would be 400 times greater than for the English-Netherlands cable; a dot would take 40 seconds to transmit. And furthermore, he said, the dot would be so spread out in time that it would be difficult to detect at the receiving end.

The chief engineer of the Atlantic Telegraph Company, which was planning to lay the cable, said that Lord Kelvin was wrong, and that practical experience showed clearly

that there would be no problem. Unfortunately, the chief
engineer was confusing submarine lines with telegraph lines.
Telegraph lines, supported on poles well above the surface of
the earth, were not subject to the same degree of retardation
as were the low-lying submarine cables separated from the
sea bottom by only the thickness of the gutta-percha insulation. Lord Kelvin's analysis of the problem stated this difference plainly, but the directors of the Atlantic Telegraph
Company discarded Lord Kelvin's prediction in favor of the
chief engineer's assurance that there would be no problem.

The cable was laid, and as the Queen's message showed
only too well, Lord Kelvin was right and the chief engineer
was wrong. In fact, if it had not been for another invention
of Lord Kelvin's, the cable would have been a total failure.

The signals arrived as Lord Kelvin had predicted—very
spread out and very weak. The devices that had been used in
the past to detect the signals were much too insensitive to
pick up the signals launched from the other side of the Atlantic. So Lord Kelvin designed a new device, which was
very sensitive to the smallest currents. His design was based
upon an idea we discussed earlier—attaching a mirror to a
moving magnet to magnify the motion of the magnet. In
Lord Kelvin's device, the moving magnet was replaced by a
very light-weight coil of wire mounted in a powerful stationary magnet. The sensitivity was magnified, as before, by the
moving spot of light reflected from the mirror mounted on
the wire coil. With Lord Kelvin's device, the messages could
be read even though transmission was weak and at a very
slow rate.

The next trans-Atlantic cable was made to Lord Kelvin's
specifications, and each piece was carefully tested before it
was accepted. Through no fault of Lord Kelvin's, this cable
also broke, however, while it was being laid.

Finally, in 1866, a cable was laid from Valentia, Ireland,

to Heart's Content, Newfoundland. The *Great Eastern,* the largest ship in the world at that time, carried the 3,088 miles of cable coiled in three cylindrical piles. As the ship reeled out the cable at the rate of about 7 miles per hour, constant contact between the ship and Valentia through the cable insured that the cable had not been damaged. This cable operated successfully for six years.

By the end of the 19th century there were a dozen cables crossing the Atlantic, and even the much wider Pacific Ocean had been crossed several times. In 1903 it was possible to send a message entirely around the world by cable and telegraph. President Theodore Roosevelt participated in the transmission of the first such message, which took nine minutes to circle the globe.

But while industry was devoting enormous amounts of time, energy, and money to the pursuit of installing submarine cables, work was going on in other laboratories of the world that was laying the foundation for an even faster form of communication—a communication without cables or wires.

6.
Spark Machines & Lines of Force

In Chapter 2 we mentioned the semaphore signals used by ships and railroads. We saw that although the signals themselves travel at the speed of light—300,000 kilometers (km) per second—the system is cumbersome and slow because spelling out the message is time consuming. The problem of slowness increases when the message must be relayed through several stations.

A semaphore system built in France in 1792, for example, required nearly 12 minutes to send a message from Toulon to Paris, a distance of less than 80 km. The system, for which its designer, Claude Chappe, coined the first use of the name *the telegraph*, was slow for several reasons. Each semaphore station consisted of a tall pole with movable blades mounted on the top. These were operated from below by a system of pulleys and ropes. As the operator manipulated the ropes, the blades moved to different positions that represented the different letters of the alphabet.

The stations were placed every 10 km or so. Before a message could be sent on to the next station, it had to be verified. To do this, the station that had just received the message sent it back to the one that had just sent it. If the message returned was correct, the first station signalled the

second to send it on to the third, and so on, to its final destination.

Since the signals traveled at the speed of light, the operator had to wait only a few millionths of a second to see a
blade move from one position to the next. So it was not the
speed with which the signals traveled that made the system
so slow. It was the reaction time of the operators and the
general awkwardness of the system.

Today most of our advanced communication systems use
radio waves for signals; and like the light waves of the semaphore system, radio waves travel at the speed of light. In
fact, according to Albert Einstein's famous Special Theory
of Relativity, no signal can travel faster than the speed of
light. So why are our present-day systems so much faster than
those of even a generation ago? It is because we know how to
transmit messages at a very high rate of speed, and we also
know how to receive and process them at very high rates.

Much has been done over the past 30 years to determine
the best and most efficient ways to send electronic messages.
Most of the time our understanding of what should be done
has been far ahead of our ability to carry it out. But with
the invention of chips, the gap between what we should
do and what we can do is narrowing rapidly. This gap between understanding and application is an old story in
science and technology. Quite often some advance in our
knowledge of nature plants the seed of a new technological
development that may take years to mature. And this brings
us back to the subject of light.

We have already learned that although nothing can
travel faster than light, the speed of light is not infinite.
Yet before 1676, many thought that light traveled instan-
taneously between two points. But in that year a Danish
astronomer conducted some clever experiments, involving
the moons of Jupiter, which clearly showed that light travels
at a very high but finite speed. The measurements indicated

a speed about two-thirds of the presently accepted value—not too bad, considering the crudeness of his measuring instruments.

Once the finite speed of light was established, scientists began to wonder why it traveled at this speed and not some other. No one had any idea. But the solution to the "problem of the speed of light" opened the door to radio communication, although no one quite understood that point at the time.

The most famous English scientist in the late 18th century was Sir Humphrey Davy. Sir Humphrey headed the prestigious Royal Institution of London, and it was there that 21-year-old Michael Faraday applied for a job as bottle washer. Thirteen years later, Faraday succeeded Davy as director. Faraday, a former bookbinder, had little formal education; and what he knew of chemistry and physics he had learned from the books he had bound as a youth. Although he was never very good at mathematics, he is considered one of the greatest experimental scientists of all time. He loved to work with things he could manipulate in his hands—things like the magnets and coils of wire that cluttered his laboratory.

One of the outstanding puzzles during Faraday's life concerned what is called the "action at a distance" problem. How was it that a magnetized compass needle could respond to the movement of a nearby magnet? Why did bits of paper jump in the vicinity of a comb just run through someone's hair? How could objects act on each other when there was nothing visible connecting them?

Faraday imagined invisible "lines of force"—electric and magnetic field lines, he called them—connecting magnetized and electrified objects like compass needles and combs charged with "static" electricity. He represented these forces as patterns of lines in graphical form; the direction of the line represented the direction of the force, and the density of the lines represented the strength of the force. The draw-

Michael Faraday
perplexed other
scientists with
his idea of invisible
electric and magnetic
"lines of force."

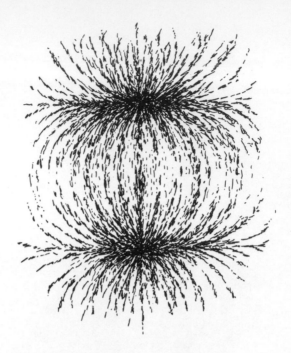

Iron filings line up along magnetic lines of force

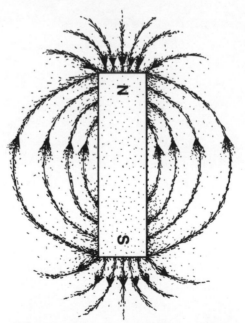

**The patterns of the iron filings describe
the lines of force for a bar magnet
fig. 1**

ings, as illustrated in Figure 1, may remind you of experiments you may have performed in science class with iron filings spread on a paper laid over a magnet. But in Faraday's time, some of his friends who greatly respected his work—particularly his work in chemistry—began to wonder if he hadn't been working too hard.

Faraday's crazy idea, however, had just what James Clerk Maxwell needed to get him started on the road to what some say turned out to be the greatest scientific achievement of the 19th century. If Faraday's knowledge of mathematics was marginal, Maxwell's equalled or surpassed the best his age had to offer. His first scientific paper was published when he was 15 years old, and at age 24 he was made professor of physics and astronomy at Cambridge University, in England. Maxwell's great achievement was to take Faraday's rather mechanical model of electric and magnetic forces and turn it into a mathematical model that still holds to this day. His theory of electricity and magnetism, like all great physical theories, not only explained the observed electrical and magnetic phenomena of his day but went further. It showed that electricity and magnetism are "two sides of the same coin," as Øersted and Ampère had suspected. But Maxwell's mathematical "marriage" of electricity and magnetism went far beyond anything Øersted and Ampère had imagined.

This marriage yielded some predictions that were entirely new and unexpected. According to Maxwell's theory, it should be possible with electric currents to generate an electrical and magnetic disturbance that could travel indefinitely through empty space. At that time no one, including Maxwell, really understood the nature of these waves. But there was one other startling prediction: Whatever the nature of these waves, they spread with the speed of light. This led Maxwell to suggest that light waves were some form of what he called "electrical and magnetic disturbance," and what we today call *electromagnetic waves*. But at the time of

James Clerk Maxwell
forecast
the existence
of radio waves.

his death in 1879, the year Albert Einstein was born, Maxwell's electromagnetic waves were still only a theoretical prediction, not an experimentally verified fact.

In that same year, the Berlin Academy offered a prize to anyone who could detect the waves predicted by Maxwell's theory. A German physicist, Heinrich Hertz, was greatly interested in the problem, but he could see no way to solve it— at least not right away. But a few years later it occurred to him that it might be possible to generate electromagnetic waves in free space.

Starting in 1866, he performed a number of brilliant experiments that proved Maxwell's theory correct. The clue to Hertz's discovery was Maxwell's assertion that electric currents should produce electromagnetic waves. Maxwell had also provided another clue: although he suspected that light was some form of electromagnetic wave, he doubted that the source of light waves could be detected. He reasoned first that the waves that make up light are at an extremely high frequency—some 10 trillion vibrations per second. He reasoned second that any object that could vibrate fast enough to produce light waves must be very small—too small to observe. Perhaps some device could be made, however, that would produce electromagnetic waves of a much lower frequency.

This was exactly the approach taken by Hertz some 20 years after Maxwell had proposed his theory. Hertz had done some experiments with a device that could produce electrical sparks across a short air gap separating two wires. What appeared to be a spark was actually a series of many brief sparks jumping back and forth between the two wires. Hertz had discovered a way to control the frequency with which the sparks jumped back and forth. This "spark machine," then, was the device he needed to produce the "lower frequency" that Maxwell suggested was necessary to detect electromagnetic waves.

Heinrich Rudolph Hertz
proved the existence
of radio waves.

Now Hertz made an interesting discovery. If he took a short piece of wire and formed it into a loop with a short gap between the two ends of the wire, a spark would jump across the short gap of the loop wire whenever a spark jumped across the wire gap of his spark machine. Figure 2 shows his mechanism. This happened even when the machine and the wire loop were separated by several feet.

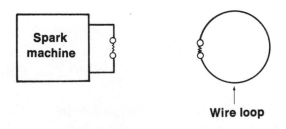

fig. 2

A spark produced by the spark machine causes an electric current in a nearby loop

This was very curious. Somehow the spark produced by his machine was causing an electric current to flow in the wire loop even though there was no visible connection between the two. Hertz was pretty sure that the invisible connection was the electromagnetic wave that Maxwell had predicted. If this was the case, then the frequency of the jumping sparks at the spark machine and at the wire loop should be the same. Hertz showed that this was, in fact, true.

The final test was to determine whether there was a short delay between a spark at the spark machine and the one produced at the wire loop, since Maxwell had predicted that electromagnetic waves spread with the speed of light. Hertz measured this delay and found that it was exactly what it should be. He was now certain that he had generated and detected the electromagnetic waves predicted by Maxwell.

Hertz did a number of other experiments that demonstrated that radiation from his spark machine had all the characteristics of light. It could be reflected by various objects and focused by metallic mirrors. These experiments and others dramatically confirmed Maxwell's theory.

A few years later, X-rays were discovered, and even later, gamma rays. We now know that these rays, as well as radio and light rays, are all forms of electromagnetic radiation. Maxwell's electromagnetic laws took their place with Sir Isaac Newton's laws of motion as one of the basic features of nature.

As we have said, Maxwell died before he saw his theory confirmed, and Hertz died without seeing his spark machine and wire loop turned into the first crude radio transmitter and receiver. It was not until 1890—well after a large part of the world had already been connected by telegraph wires and submarine cables—that it occurred to anyone that Maxwell's electromagnetic waves could be used for communication.

7.
They Said It Couldn't Be Done

Most of the men associated with early developments in the science of electricity and magnetism—men like Øersted, Ampère, Faraday, and Maxwell—pursued their studies purely for the sake of understanding nature. They were not particularly interested in the practical implications of their work. What role Hertz might have played in the development of radio is hard to say because he died in 1894 at age 36, shortly after publication of his great textbook on electricity, titled *Electric Waves*, in the English edition.

But if Hertz did not see or care about the commercial possibilities of his work during his lifetime, others did. In a letter dated December 1, 1889, an engineer who was working at an electric power generating station in the Netherlands wrote to Hertz asking about the possibility of transmitting the "invisible magnetic lines of force across a distance." The engineer enclosed a sketch of how he thought the system might work.

Hertz replied two days later. His response was directed at the specific system the engineer had proposed, pointing out several practical difficulties, not the least of which was that the "receiving and transmitting mirrors" would have to be about 300 km in diameter.

Whatever feelings Hertz had about "wireless" communication, his discoveries were the key to its development. Three years after Hertz's death, Sir William Crookes, an English chemist, wrote an article titled "Some Possibilities of Electricity" for a popular London magazine. In it he proposed using electromagnetic waves for telegraphy.

Considering the fact that no actual radio broadcast system existed at that time, Crookes's article was amazingly accurate in its analysis of the benefits and shortcomings of radio. He realized the need for transmitters that would transmit at a single frequency. The Hertz spark machine emitted a signal over a whole range of frequencies, as does the radio signal generated by a nearby lightning flash, the "crash" of which can be heard at almost any point on the AM radio dial. Without this single-frequency feature, every station would interfere with every other station. And for the same reason, there would have to be radio receivers that would tune in just the frequency of the desired radio station; they would also need to be far more sensitive than the wire loop used by Hertz.

Crookes also touched upon a problem we mentioned in Chapter 2: how could the lanterns be seen on a foggy night? In his article, Crookes wrote, "Rays of light will not pierce through a wall, nor as we know only too well, through a London fog. But the electrical vibrations of a yard or more in wavelength of which I have spoken will easily pierce such mediums, which to them will be transparent."

But Crookes, like most of the professional scientists of his time, was interested in a number of different investigations at the same time, and he probably did not have time to pursue his suggestion. In fact, being a scientist may have been a disadvantage because the prevailing scientific belief at the time was that the radio waves traveled like beams of light, in straight lines; the curvature of the earth's surface would make long-distance radio communication impossible.

While many of the world's most distinguished scientists were questioning the feasibility of radio communication, a young Italian, Guglielmo Marconi, was trying to join the Italian navy as an officer; he was turned down because he was not considered smart enough. Later he tried to enter the University of Bologna, but was again rejected on the same grounds. But he did manage to persuade the university authorities to allow him to attend a series of physics lectures that included some material about Hertz's experiments.

Marconi immediately hit upon the idea that the "Hertz apparatus" could be used for "wireless" communication. Within weeks he had put together the necessary equipment and was conducting experiments on his father's estate near Pontecchio, Italy. Later Marconi wrote that he could "scarcely conceive it possible that their (radio waves) application to useful purposes could have escaped the notice of eminent scientists."

Marconi began his experiments in 1895, and by the end of that year he had succeeded in establishing communication over a distance of 2.4 km. During this period he made several improvements to the Hertz system. First he added an antenna to his transmitter. With this addition he was able to signal across the entire length of his father's garden, a few hundred meters, and he further discovered that the signal distance increased as he increased the height of his antenna.

Another important improvement concerned what was known at the time as the "coherer." The coherer was the part of the receiving apparatus that detected the presence of a radio signal. When a signal was present, the coherer acted like a switch, which closed to activate a device that made a mark on a piece of paper.

When Marconi could not interest the Italian government in his tests, his mother suggested that his system would find its best application for communication with ships, where wire links with land were impossible. Marconi accepted his mother's suggestion and moved his equipment to England, the world's greatest sea power at that time.

In 1896, he demonstrated his system to British Post Office officials, who immediately saw its significance. By the end of that year he had extended his signal distance to 15 km, over the Salisbury Plain of England; and the next year he formed The Marconi Wireless and Signal Company, Ltd.

Surprisingly, the telegraph companies did not see the Marconi system as competition. Since anyone within range of the signal could pick up the messages, it lacked the privacy of the wired systems, and telegraph company owners saw Marconi's wireless as useful mainly for over-water communication.

Marconi continued to improve his system; by the summer of 1899, he had exchanged messages over sea paths longer than 100 km. The next year he again confounded the scientific community by stating that he was preparing facilities to communicate by wireless across the Atlantic Ocean. As we said, scientists were convinced that radio waves traveled in straight lines, and that communication over such vast distances was a scientific impossibility. But the scientists had been wrong before, and Marconi thought he might prove them wrong again.

It took more than a year to set up the necessary equipment in England and the United States. The English site was in Cornwall, near the southwestern tip of England; and the American site was on Cape Cod, Massachusetts. Just after the antennas had been erected in September of 1901, a storm swept the Atlantic and knocked down the antennas on both sides of the ocean.

A new temporary antenna was quickly rebuilt in England; and in November, Marconi sailed with a group of assistants to Newfoundland, where they established a site at Signal Hill, near St. John's. Instead of stringing his new antenna between poles sunk in the ground, Marconi decided

Guglielmo Marconi (left)
proved the scientists wrong.

to hoist it with a kite. Once the Newfoundland site was established, he sent a cablegram to England instructing the crew at the Cornwall site to begin sending the letter *s*, in Morse code: · · · , between 3:00 and 6:00 p.m. each day. The next day, December 12, 1901, Marconi heard the coded signal faintly, but not on a regular basis. We know now that the signal faded in and out because the kite moved up and down in the winds. This had the effect of changing the tuning frequency of his radio receiver; part of the time the receiver was tuned to the incoming signal, and part of the time it was not.

News of Marconi's achievement swept the world, and at

age 27 he had become an almost legendary figure. Even *The New York Times* pointed out that Marconi had succeeded in spite of obstacles projected by the scientific community.

Marconi's achievement was typical of the early history of the development of electrical communication. Many times the "working device" had no adequate theoretical explanation. In fact, the mere existence of a particular device often spurred basic scientific research, which in turn often led to a deeper understanding of the whole area of science. Marconi's transatlantic radio communication made scientists reexamine their views of the behavior of radio waves, and this led to discovery of the ionosphere—about which we shall learn more later. As we shall see in Chapter 10, the discovery of the electron, which revolutionized electrical communication, is another example of this sequence of events.

8.
Talking Through a Wire

Telegraph wires and undersea cables were tremendously important strands in man's growing communication web. They had cut communication time between the east and west coast of the United States from weeks to just minutes, and had bound together old-world Europe and new-world America. But it was still a chore to translate the Morse code into letters and words.

An idea for the possibility of sending speech directly over a wire came through a misunderstanding. Alexander Graham Bell, born in Edinburgh, Scotland, in 1847, was the son of an elocution teacher. Perhaps because of his father's influence, young Bell also became interested in the study of speech, and particularly in the communication problems of the deaf.

In his studies, Bell came across a book by a German scientist, Herman von Helmholz, that described some of his experiments using electrically driven tuning forks to produce vowel sounds mechanically. Bell didn't read German very well, and he mistakenly thought that Helmholz was sending vowel sounds over a wire. Eventually Bell became aware of his mistake, but he continued to be fascinated with the idea of speech communication over a wire.

Before he was able to pursue his idea, however, tragedy

struck his family. Both his brothers died of tuberculosis, and Bell himself seemed to be affected. Hoping to save his only surviving son, Bell's father decided to move his family to Canada.

During his recuperation in Canada, Bell started reading Helmholz's book again, this time in a French translation which he could understand more easily. Although Bell's knowledge of anatomy and physiology was extensive, he had little knowledge of physics. So he read Helmholz's book many times, gradually gaining some understanding of electricity and magnetism. He also continued his work with the deaf, and eventually become professor of "vocal physiology and elocution" at Boston University.

This appointment was fortunate for several reasons. First, Bell had an opportunity to extend his knowledge of physics through discussions with the physicist Joseph Henry at the nearby Smithsonian Institution, in Washington, D.C. It was Henry, you may recall, who helped Morse develop the relay for his telegraph system. Second, Boston was a center for manufacturing telegraph equipment, and so Bell had easy access to a good deal of skilled help. And finally, Bell was able to find needed financial backing there.

Although he was fully aware by now that he had misunderstood Helmholz's book, Bell's first attempts at voice communication over a wire were modeled around Helmholz's work. His first idea was to install several tuning forks at both ends of the wire path. At the transmission end he hoped to generate several electrical signals; the frequency of each would correspond to the frequency of a tuning fork at this end. His plan was that each of these electrical signals would cause the corresponding tuning fork at the receiving end to vibrate. He hoped by this means to be able to send several telegraph signals at the same time over a single wire.

Although his plan solved the problem of sending multiple signals over the same wire, it was not the solution for transmitting the human voice, since the voice consists of a continuous range of frequencies and not just steady tones at a few specific frequencies.

At this point Bell contacted Henry and explained his problem. Henry recalled a device he had been asked to examine in 1846. Called a "talking figure," it was capable of speaking words and even whole sentences that could be clearly understood. The device was operated manually from a keyboard, which was in turn attached to a system of strings and levers that controlled the operations of a number of "artificial organs" making up the speech apparatus of the talking figure. It occurred to Henry at the time that the keyboard could be replaced with a series of electromagnets that could move in response to signals sent over a telegraph line. In effect, then, one could operate a talking figure by remote control over a telegraph line, or even across the Atlantic by cable.

Bell continued his work with tuning forks, but finally replaced them with magnetized metal reeds from pipe organs. At this point his knowledge of anatomy came to his aid. He attached one end of the reed to a thin metal diaphragm so that the reed-diaphragm arrangement was somewhat similar to the construction of the human ear. He reasoned that the sound waves generated by the spoken word would cause the diaphragm to vibrate, and this in turn would cause the reed to vibrate. Then as the reed vibrated near an electromagnet, the electromagnet would generate an electric current whose fluctuations followed the vibrations of the diaphragm. In the next chapter we shall discuss more fully how electromagnets operate.

At the receiving end, Bell planned to operate this device backwards. There the fluctuating current would arrive by the copper wire, pass through the windings of the electro-

When Alexander Graham Bell invented the telephone, no one thought it would ever be very useful.

magnet, and produce a fluctuating magnetic field, which would cause the magnetized reed to vibrate. As the reed vibrated, it would move the diaphragm against the surrounding air, producing sound that mimicked the sound at the transmission end.

By June of 1875, Bell had perfected his system. His assistant, John Watson, plucked the reed at the transmitting end, sending a fluctuating current down the wire to Bell, who was at the other end with another reed-diaphragm device pressed tightly to his ear. At first there was just the one device at each end, which served as either transmitter or receiver, like the tin-can telephones you and your friends may have constructed when you were children. The twanging sound of the reed emerged clearly from Bell's "receiver." A day later Bell had the system transmitting speech sounds, and by March of the following year he sent the first complete sentence—the now well-known "Mr. Watson, come here; I want you"—through his instrument to his assistant in the next room. He was awarded his first patent on March 7, 1876, four days after his 29th birthday.

As news of Bell's invention spread, the Western Union Company became concerned that his telephone would be a serious threat to the telegraph. So to keep from having to pay for the use of Bell's invention, the Western Union Company hired a young inventor to create a new kind of telephone transmitter. The inventor, Thomas A. Edison, soon came up with a new approach that was superior to Bell's. Like Bell's transmitter, Edison's device converted sound waves to electrical waves; but it was based on a new principle.

Edison's transmitter consisted of a small box filled with carbon particles. One side of the box was covered with a thin metal diaphragm that fluctuated back and forth in the presence of sound waves. As the diaphragm moved in, it compressed the carbon particles, decreasing their resistance to

Thomas Alva Edison invented many electrical devices, largely by trial and error.

electric current flow; and when the diaphragm moved out, the pressure on the carbon particles decreased, resulting in greater resistance to the flow of the electric current. When a caller lifted the telephone from its hook, a current from a battery flowed through the carbon particles. As the caller spoke into the device, the diaphragm vibrated back and forth, causing the current flowing through the carbon particles to fluctuate in step with the speaker's voice.

Claims by inventors and applications for patents resulted in a deluge of law suits. To avoid prolonging the court battles, the Bell Company and the Western Union Company agreed in 1879 that the Bell Company would not establish a telegraph service and that the Western Union Company would stay out of the telephone business. Further, the Western Union Company agreed to turn over its patent rights to the Edison transmitter for "certain sums of money" to be paid by the Bell Company over the next 17 years.

Although it's hard to imagine our homes and communities without telephones today, people were not enthusiastic about the new invention. Most saw it as a gadget or novelty that would probably never have much use. There was no central exchange, and early promoters lent or rented telephones to prospective customers in pairs—perhaps much as walkie-talkie radios in the toy store or radio shop are packaged today. People who acquired a pair of phones could then arrange for their own connection between neighbors or between home and office or store, or wherever they wished. The Bell Company had big plans for a telephone system, but they had a hard time finding people with enough faith in their plans to put money into building the system.

To some extent the existing telegraph system provided a guide for installing a telephone system, but there was a crucial difference. To serve its purpose, a telephone system required that any telephone in the system could be connected to any other. This necessity created an entirely new problem—the problem of providing a central exchange with a system of switches.

The first commercial switchboard was built in New Haven, Connecticut, in 1878. It connected a total of 21 telephones, and the switching was done manually by telephone operators at switching centers. Today the switching is done automatically by electromechanical devices, and in the latest systems by computers.

With the problem of switching under control, the telephone system grew rapidly. By 1880, there were nearly 50,000 subscribers, and by 1885, nearly 156,000. Most major cities had telephone systems, and many cities had connections to other cities. But the system came up against the same problem that had stopped the spread of the telegraph: How could people put telephone lines across the sea?

The answer might seem simple at first. Why not just route the telephone calls through the existing submarine cables? But unfortunately there's a vast difference between telephone signals and telegraph signals. Telegraph signals are very simple, consisting basically of short and long on-off impulses, whereas telephone signals are complex, reflecting the complexity of human voice patterns. The submarine cables had been designed to carry the relatively sluggish pulses of the Morse code, and would completely distort voice signals.

There was also the problem of amplification. For all practical purposes, a telephone signal would have vanished by the time it crossed the ocean through a submarine cable. What was needed was some system of amplifiers placed at regular intervals along a submarine cable. But at that time no such amplifiers existed, and no one knew how to build them.

The first transatlantic phone call was not made until

1915, and then it spanned the ocean by radio, not by cable. The first transmitters and receivers were located at Arlington, Virginia, and at the Eiffel Tower in Paris; and the system was called radio-telephone. It was not until 1956, some 90 years after the first successful transatlantic telegraph cable was laid, that overseas telephone communication by cable was possible.

9.
Nature's Symmetry

Up to this point we have looked at the growth of the communication web as it took place historically. Many different persons from different backgrounds contributed to the developments. Some, like Marconi and Bell, had little education in the physical sciences. They simply tried one arrangement and another until they found something that worked. Often they had no idea why or how it worked. Others, like Maxwell and Hertz, had no practical goals in mind; they wished only to further man's understanding of the physical world. Such men were interested in the possibility that some underlying laws of nature must govern all electrical phenomena, and they tried to define these laws.

To understand better the systems we have looked at thus far—and to lay a better foundation for understanding the more complex systems we shall examine later—let's pause in our historical account to think about electricity and magnetism and the laws of nature. Some of this chapter may seem difficult, but it need not be if you just keep the two terms *electric* and *magnetic* in mind and make a distinction between the two.

The main features of all electrical communication systems can be explained by just four basic laws of electricity and magnetism. We met the first of these laws in Chapter 4, where we discussed Øersted's experiments with a compass and current-carry wire:

1. *Electrical currents produce magnetic lines of force that circle the conductor.*

This law suggests another possibility: If electric currents can produce magnetic fields, perhaps magnetic fields can produce electric currents. This kind of *symmetry* often occurs in the laws of nature. One of the persons who investigated this possibility was Michael Faraday, who, you perhaps recall, introduced the idea of electric and magnetic fields that Maxwell found so useful in developing his theory.

Faraday had tried many different arrangements of wires and magnets, but he could detect no currents flowing in the wires. Øersted's experiment had demonstrated that a steady current in a wire produces a steady magnetic field. But the opposite did not seem to be true; a steady magnetic field did not produce a steady current in a wire.

The solution to this problem came to Faraday in 1831, largely by accident. He was experimenting with two insulated wires wound on an iron ring, as shown in Figure 1. One wire was connected to a battery, and the other to a meter that measured electric current, an *ammeter*. Although there was no electrical connection between the two wires, he noticed that when he either closed or opened the switch, the current flowed.

As we know, when a current flows it produces a magnetic field. In this particular arrangement, the magnetic field created by the current flowing in coiled wire A produces a magnetic field that is guided by the iron ring, so that it passes through the coiled loops of wire B. Before the switch is closed, there is no magnetic field; but the instant the switch is closed, a magnetic field quickly builds up. It was during this build-up period that the current flowed in wire

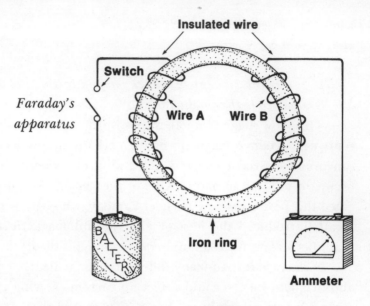

Insulated wire

Switch

Faraday's apparatus

Wire A   Wire B

BATTERY

Iron ring

Ammeter

fig. 1

B. Similarly, when the switch is opened, the magnetic field produced by wire A quickly collapses because a current no longer flows.

Faraday soon realized that what was necessary to produce an electric current was a *changing* magnetic field. A *steady* magnetic field would not produce a current; but by continually closing and opening the switch connecting wire A to the battery, he could cause a current to flow back and forth in wire B.

He also found, as he had suspected, that a changing magnetic field produced by a magnet causes a current to flow. Figure 2 shows how he demonstrated this principle. Simply by moving a magnet in and out of the coil of wire, he could cause a current to flow in wire C. We can summarize Faraday's experiments to give us our second general law of electricity and magnetism:

> 2. *A changing magnetic field causes a current to flow in a conductor.*

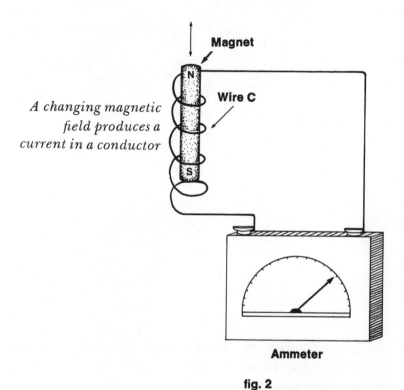

Magnet

N

Wire C

A changing magnetic field produces a current in a conductor

S

Ammeter

fig. 2

Laws 1 and 2 do not seem to have the kind of symmetry we might expect. A *steady* current produces a magnetic field, whereas a *changing* magnetic field produces a current.

This was the situation that confronted Maxwell in the 1860s as he thought about electricity and magnetism. He felt sure that nature was not "lopsided"—that there should be a greater symmetry between electricity and magnetism. Some kind of changing "electric phenomena" should produce a magnetic field.

At this point he introduced an entirely new and far-reaching idea. He said a changing "electric *field*" should produce a magnetic *field,* as well as a current in a conductor.

Figure 3 shows how we can create such a changing electric field. Suppose we connect a battery to a pair of conducting plates separated by an air gap. If we close the switch

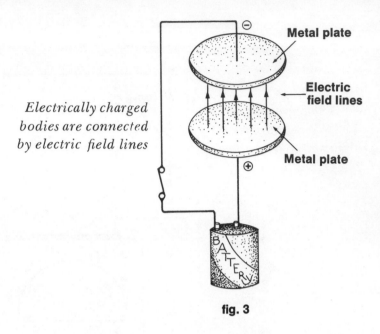

Electrically charged bodies are connected by electric field lines

- Metal plate
- Electric field lines
- Metal plate

fig. 3

to the battery, current flows toward the plates; but because of the gap the current is stopped, so positive and negative charges "pile up" on the two plates. But these negative and positive charges are connected by electric field lines, according to Faraday's idea that magnetized and electrically charged bodies are connected by magnetic field lines and electric field lines.

When we first close the switch, the charges begin to pile up on the plates; and as the charges accumulate, the electric field lines increase in strength, producing an electric field that is changing in strength. According to Maxwell, this changing electric field should produce a magnetic field. Thus Maxwell's third law:

3. Changing electric fields in space produce magnetic fields.

Now, we already know from Law 2 that a changing magnetic field produces a current in a conductor. But suppose there is no conductor near the changing magnetic field. Does that mean that nothing is happening? Perhaps it is more likely that a changing magnetic field produces an electric field; and then if a conductor is present, it is this electric field that causes the current to flow in the wire. So Maxwell added a fourth and final general law of electricity and magnetism:

4. *Changing magnetic fields in space produce electric fields.*

Laws 3 and 4 have the symmetry that Maxwell was searching for.

Let's restate all four together, where we can refer to them easily if we wish:

1. Electrical currents produce magnetic lines of force that circle the conductor.
2. A changing magnetic field causes a current to flow in a conductor.
3. Changing electric fields in space produce magnetic fields.
4. Changing magnetic fields in space produce electric fields.

As we said in Chapter 6, Maxwell converted these laws into a mathematical model that predicted the existence of radio waves. But before we return to that subject, let's go back briefly to see how we can use the laws to understand the electrical communication systems we've been talking about in the last few chapters.

Figure 4 shows that Law 1 is all we need to explain the operation of a telegraph. We simply close a telegraph key momentarily, sending a pulse through the telegraph wire. At the receiver end, the pulse flows in a coil of wire, producing a magnetic field. Usually the coil is wound on an iron core, which has the effect of concentrating the magnetic field lines.

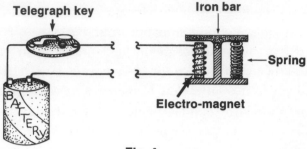

Fig. 4

The telegraph is based on Law 1

The arrangement of coil and iron core is called an *electromagnet* because it produces a magnetic field when an electrical current flows in it.

If we place a small, spring-loaded iron bar over the top of the electromagnet as shown in the figure, the electromagnet will pull the bar down against the restraining tug of the spring. And if we adjust the strength of the spring properly, the pull of the electromagnet will be just enough to cause the bar to swing down and tap the top of the electromagnet. Then when the current stops, the spring will return the bar to its initial position. By having keys and electromagnets at both ends of the path, we can send and receive messages through the same wires.

The telephone is just a sophisticated version of the telegraph, in which the "on-off" currents are replaced by a continuously varying current that follows the vibrations in the sound of the speaker's voice. As we explained in the previous chapter, the changing current is produced at the transmission end by sending a current through a small volume of carbon particles whose resistance to current flow is changed by the vibrating motion of the diaphragm of the mouthpiece, or transmitter. When the changing current reaches the receiving end, it flows through an electromagnet, causing the strength of the electromagnet to fluctuate in step with the changing current. This causes the metal diaphragm to vibrate, producing a sound that mimics the voice of the speaker.

Now let's use our laws to tackle the more mysterious problem of communication by radio waves. We'll start by imagining a chain—a very odd chain with alternating links of copper and glass. As we know, glass is a nonconductor; so no electric current can flow from one copper link to the next copper link. The first and last links are of copper, as shown in Figure 5.

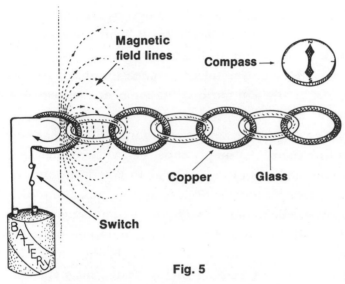

Fig. 5

Laws 1 and 2 operate together

We'll cut a small section of copper from the first link and connect the ends of the severed link to the terminals of a battery; and we'll insert a switch in one of the wires leading to the battery. When we close the switch, a current circulates in the first link, producing a magnetic field according to Law 1. As the current builds up to its strongest value, the magnetic field also builds up to a steady value.

As we know from Law 2, a changing magnetic field causes a current to flow in a conductor. Since the second copper link in the chain is near the first one, part of the changing magnetic field produced by the first link will pass through the second copper link, causing a current to flow in it. But at the point when the magnetic field in the first link reaches its steady value, the current in the second copper link will stop.

We know from Law 1 that the current flowing in the second copper link will also produce a magnetic field, and part of this field will thread through the third copper link. And again, as the current in the second link builds up and collapses, it will produce a changing magnetic field that will cause a current to flow in the third. This process continues from one copper link to the next until the last link in the chain is involved. If we place a compass near this last copper link, the needle will move at the moment the current starts to flow in this link.

We now have a way to communicate over our copper-glass link chain. We simply close the switch at the transmission end, and this causes a signal to flow from one copper link to the next until it reaches the last link and causes the compass needle to move. We notice that although the switch is closed during this whole process, only one pulse travels down the chain. If we open the switch, the current in the first link dies out, causing the associated magnetic field to collapse, and thus launches another pulse throughout the chain.

This isn't quite a radio wave, but it is close, since we have been able to communicate between two points not connected by any continuous wire. Now, we wonder, is it really necessary to have the copper links between the first and last copper links? The answer is no, because of Laws 3 and 4. We know from Law 4 that the reason a current flows in the second copper link after we close the switch is that the changing magnetic field produced by the first link sets up an electric field in space. And it is this electric field that causes the current to flow in the second copper link. But from Law 3, a changing electric field in space produces a magnetic field. So we can dispense with the intermediate copper links because the interlocking changing electric and magnetic fields are sufficient to generate each other. So our interlocking *electromagnetic waves* propagate in free space from the sending copper link attached to the battery to the receiving link placed near a compass.

Let's go one step further. Suppose we take the copper link at the transmission end and straighten it out, as shown in Figure 6. Now it looks like a radio transmitter antenna. We can also cut and straighten the copper link at the receiv-

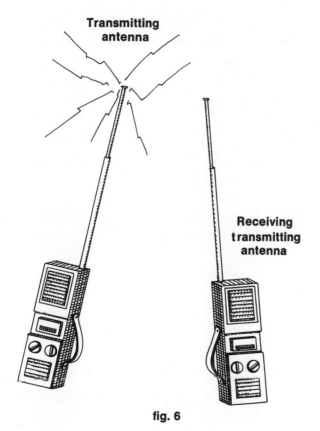

Transmitting
antenna

Receiving
transmitting
antenna

fig. 6

All four laws are needed to explain radio waves

ing end, so that it now looks like a receiving antenna. The two antennas are, in fact, identical; so if we have batteries and compasses at both ends of the path, we can transmit and receive in both directions.

It should be noted here that of course the radio waves do not travel in just a single path, as our imaginary chain might suggest. They radiate in all directions from the transmitting antenna and can be picked up by any number of receiving antennas within range of the transmitter.

Over the years many improvements have been made to this simple radio transmission system. Improvements such as transmitting at a single frequency or focusing broadcasts in a certain direction by using properly "shaped" antennas. But the system we have discussed has all of the essential features of any radio broadcast system, whether it is from a radio station, a TV station, or a satellite.

Maxwell's mathematical laws of electromagnetic waves —or *Maxwell's equations,* as they are usually called—have not been changed or improved upon to this day, and they even anticipate some of the essential features of Einstein's "Special Theory of Relativity," which was not developed until the beginning of the 20th century.

10.
Discovery of the Electron

James Maxwell had neatly bundled up the laws of electricity and magnetism into a compact package that not only explained the electrical-magnetic phenomena that had been observed, but also predicted electromagnetic waves. There was only one problem: Nobody knew exactly what electricity was. Some thought it consisted of small, electrically charged particles; others thought it was continuous and fluid-like. Many didn't know at all.

As so often happens in science, the beginning to the solution of the problem came from an apparently unrelated development. A German physicist, Heinrich Geissler, invented a vacuum pump that could reduce the pressure inside a tube of glass to less than 0.01 percent of normal air pressure. One of his friends, Julius Plücker, took one of Geissler's tubes and sealed a wire into each end. He attached a metal disc, which today we call an *electrode,* to each of the two wires that protruded into the glass; and to the two ends that protruded to the outside, he connected a battery and an ammeter, as shown in Figure 1.

Much to his surprise, Plücker discovered that electricity could flow through the nearly empty glass tube. He and one of his students also noticed that while the current flowed, the glass tube gave off a pale green glow.

Although this observation was made in 1855, very lit-

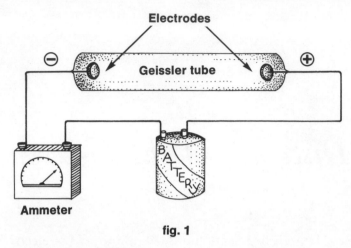

Geissler tube

Ammeter

fig. 1

*Plücker discovered that electricity could flow through
a vacuum*

tle more developed until 1875, when Sir William Crookes
conducted similar experiments. Crookes, who as we recall
from Chapter 7 had so aptly seen the possibility of radio
communication, was one of the scientists who believed that
electricity consisted of charged particles; and he was searching for a way to test his theory.

In one of his experiments, he bent a Geissler tube into
an L-shape, as shown in Figure 2. And when he connected a
battery to the tube, the green glow appeared at the bend in
the tube, opposite the electrode that was connected to the
negative terminal of the battery.

Next Crookes placed a small, cross-shaped obstruction in
the tube, in front of the negative electrode; and he noticed
that a shadow, shaped like the cross, appeared in the green
glow at the end of the tube. It was as if the negative electrode was emitting some kind of rays that could be blocked
by an obstruction that left a shadow on the tube. Knowing
that magnets have an effect on charged particles, Crookes
held a magnet near the tube. This caused the shadow to shift,
apparently because the direction of the rays had been altered
by the magnet.

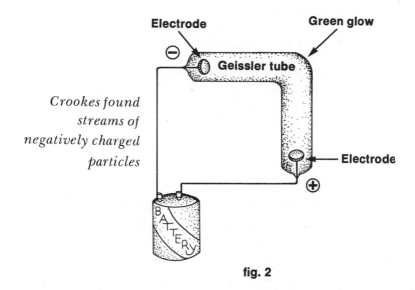

Electrode

Green glow

Geissler tube

Crookes found streams of negatively charged particles

Electrode

fig. 2

In another experiment, Crookes placed in the tube a tiny mica paddle wheel that turned when the battery was connected to send a current through the tube. He was now convinced that the rays emitted by the negatively charged electrode were streams of negatively charged particles.

Other scientists made similar experiments that verified Crookes' result, and the rays came to be called *cathode rays* because the electrode connected to the negative terminal of the battery was called the "cathode."

If electricity really consisted of negatively charged particles, a natural question was, how much does each particle weigh, and how much negative charge does it carry? This question was partially answered by another English physicist, J. J. Thomson, in 1897. Thomson knew, as did other physicists by that time, that charged particles are affected by electric and magnetic fields. He reasoned that, with "the proper arrangement" of his apparatus, he should be able to balance the electric and magnetic forces on the cathode-ray particles. His mathematical equations indicated that when this balance was achieved, he would be able to determine the ratio of the charge on the particle to its weight or mass.

With a different technique, a similar ratio had previously been obtained for the hydrogen atom. At that time it was thought that the hydrogen atom was the simplest and smallest "chunk" of matter possible. Normally hydrogen atoms—or any other atoms—do not have any electrical charge. But under some conditions they do, and it was of this "peculiar kind" of charged atom called an *ion* that the charge-to-mass ratio measurement had been made.

Thomson's experiment showed him that the charge-to-mass ratio of the cathode-ray particle was 1,800 times greater than the charge-to-mass ratio of the hydrogen atom. There was only one thing he could conclude from these results: Either the charge of a cathode-ray particle was considerably greater than that of a hydrogen atom, or the cathode-ray particle had a mass considerably smaller than that of the hydrogen atom.

Thomson did some further experiments involving different apparatus, and finally concluded that the size of the charge of the hydrogen atom was the same as or similar to that of the cathode-ray particle, and that therefore the mass of the cathode-ray particle must be about 1,800 times less than the mass of the hydrogen atom.

Thomson then proposed that there was a new kind of "elementary particle," much smaller than the hydrogen atom, and that this particle was one of the building blocks of matter. He even speculated that normal atoms consist of these elementary, negatively charged particles, in just the right proportion to offset whatever positive charge the atom might have, so that the net electrical charge of the atom is zero. Thomson's model of the atom, as shown in Figure 3, was called the "plum pudding" model because the negatively charged particles were thought to be distributed like raisins throughout the interior of the uniformly, positively charged material that made up the rest of the atom.

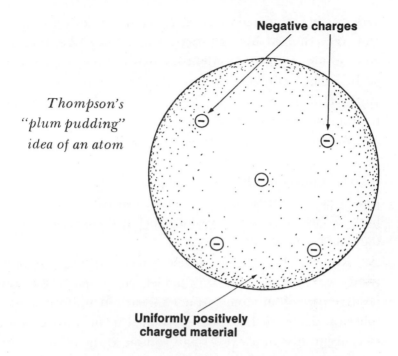

Negative charges

Thompson's "plum pudding" idea of an atom

Uniformly positively charged material

fig. 3

Although Thomson's model of the atom proved to be wrong, he was correct in his belief that cathode rays consist of very tiny negatively charged particles, which today we call *electrons*. And it is these electrons flowing through wire or space that produce an electric current. As we shall see in later chapters, Thomson's discovery of the electron was the key that allowed radio to go well beyond what seemed possible in the early days of the Marconi radio system.

Thomson's 1904 plum-pudding model of the atom stimulated many experiments to determine its structure. Answers came over a period of about three years, starting in 1909. A young New Zealand scientist, Ernest Rutherford, went to England to work in the laboratories headed by Thomson at Cambridge University, Rutherford was greatly interested in a newly discovered kind of particle called an *alpha* particle. Although it wasn't clear what these particles were, they were very massive compared to the electron, had a positive charge, and were emitted by "radioactive" materials like uranium and radium. In fact, we might say that the particles seemed to be "shot" out of radioactive materials. It occurred to Rutherford that these alpha-particle "bullets" could be used to probe the interior of the atom.

If Thomson's plum-pudding model was correct, the heavy alpha particles should pass through the atom with little or no difficulty. But during the experiments, the unexpected happened. Some of the alpha particles shot straight back in the direction from which they had come, as though they had bounced from a rock.

Rutherford quickly realized that something was drastically wrong with Thomson's model. He proposed that the positive part of an atom was not spread out uniformly in a spherical shape, as Thomson envisioned it, but in fact must be concentrated into a very small volume at the center of the atom; only such a concentrated volume of positive charge could produce the "backward bounding" alpha particles. Rutherford also proposed that the electrons making up the atom circled around the small positive core, now called the *nucleus*, as shown in Figure 4. Later we shall return to this new model of the atom and see how it set the stage for a wealth of new communication devices such as transistors and chips.

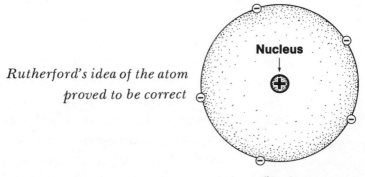

Rutherford's idea of the atom proved to be correct

Nucleus

fig. 4

11.
Dr. Appleton's Electronic Mirror

We recall that Marconi startled the scientific world in 1901 by sending radio signals across the Atlantic Ocean. The long-distance signals would have been impossible without the electron, whose discovery we have just explored. Now we need to go back and pick up some loose threads in our story.

On February 2, 1900, nearly two years before his transatlantic experiments, Marconi gave a lecture before the Royal Institution in London, describing some of his over-water experiments. In one experiment he was able to send a signal farther than 140 km, a distance clearly beyond what was possible if radio signals traveled only in straight lines. He explained that because of the earth's curvature there was "a hill of water 1,000 feet high between the transmitter and the receiver," and that "the Hertzian waves either go over or around the dome of water or pass through it." Figure 1 shows this idea.

Marconi performed other experiments that indicated unquestionably that radio signals could be received beyond "line of sight" distances; and for these reasons probably more than any others, he undertook the transatlantic project. After that success he went on experimenting and obtained some

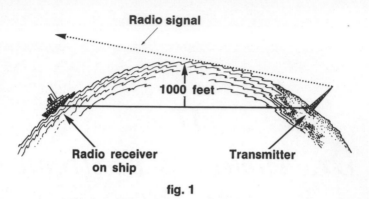

fig. 1

The earth's curvature makes a "hill of water" between transmitter and receiver.

puzzling results. First he noticed that at distances greatei than 1,100 km, signals sent during the daytime "entirely failed, whereas those sent at night remained quite strong." At distances shorter than 1,100 km, there was no apparent change in day-to-night strengths of the signals.

If Marconi had been more scientifically inclined, he might have pursued these puzzling results, but his interest lay in practical wireless communication, not in scientific curiosities. So in spite of having no adequate explanation for long-distance radio communication, he continued to expand his company. By 1919 there were 14 transmitting stations on the British coast, and nearly 6,000 ships had been fitted with wireless equipment.

One event in particular furthered the cause of ship-to-shore communication. While on her maiden voyage in April, 1912, the *Titanic,* then the world's largest ship, collided with an iceberg in the mid-Atlantic and sank with a loss of 1,500 lives. But another 700 were saved because the *Titanic* was outfitted with wireless equipment and could signal for help.

In 1902, the year following Marconi's transatlantic transmission, a British mathematician, Oliver Heaviside, and an American scientist, Arthur Kennelly, independently suggested that radio signals do not travel straight into outer space but are reflected back to the earth by a "mirror" in the upper atmosphere, as shown in Figure 2. Both men believed the mirror was due to an electrical conducting region in the atmosphere, and Heaviside further suggested that the mirror was produced by radiation from the sun.

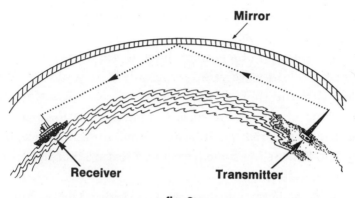

fig. 2

Some scientists thought radio signals were reflected by a mirror in the upper atmosphere

Very few people took notice of the Kennelly-Heaviside suggestion, and most communication engineers considered the atmospheric mirror—if it existed— to be a nuisance. As they saw it, the signals reflected from the mirror would interfere with the "main signal," which they believed somehow "slid along" the surface of the earth. They further believed that signals at low frequencies would cling to the earth better than would those at higher frequencies. In fact, this belief was so firmly held that in 1912 frequencies below one and a half million cycles per second—1,500 kilocycles per second—were reserved for commercial and government broadcasts, while the amateur radio operators were given the "useless" frequencies above 1,500 kilocycles per second.

During World War I, many soldiers were trained as

wireless operators; and when the war was over, many of them returned home to pursue amateur radio enthusiastically in the "useless" high-frequency range—the *short-wave band,* as it was called by then. The amateurs soon discovered, contrary to the prevailing opinion, that long-distance communication was possible in the short-wave band. It was not only possible, but could be achieved with equipment that was far less expensive and used much less power than was required at the lower frequencies.

Marconi and others were quick to see the economic advantage of short-wave radio—especially if it could be established that the short-wave, long-distance contacts were not some kind of rare occurrence. Commercial radio operators, who had considered the atmospheric mirror a nuisance, now began to hope it was some permanent feature that they could count on.

Scientists began to look at Heaviside's and Kennelly's earlier suggestions, as well as some other work done during the intervening years, with revived interest. An English scientist, W. H. Eccles, studied the theory of what happens to radio waves as they pass through electrical-conducting atmosphere. He showed how the frequency of the wave and the electrical properties of the atmospheric mirror could determine the reflection of the wave back to earth. Eccles also suggested that the mirror could be produced by ultraviolet radiation from the sun interacting with the rarefied air in the upper atmosphere.

On the night of December 11, 1924, Marconi, who had just been elected President of the Royal Society of Arts, was giving his inaugural address in London. In it he said, "It is my belief that the whole theory and practice of long-distance wireless communication is just now undergoing a most important and radical change."

At almost the same hour, two young scientists, Dr. Edward Victor Appleton and Miles Barnett, were on their way to Oxford to set up equipment for an experiment to be conducted the following night—an experiment that started Appleton on the path to a Nobel prize in physics more than two decades later.

In 1911, Appleton was a student at Cambridge University, where one of his favorite professors was J. J. Thomson, the discoverer of the electron. Shortly after Appleton's graduation, England declared war on Germany and he joined the Army as a private. Later promoted to officer's rank, he was sent to the British Army's first "radio school." Almost as soon as the course had started, the instructor became ill and Appleton was asked to take over the class. This chance incident kept him from being shipped to the battle front and initiated his lifelong interest in radio.

After the war Appleton returned to Cambridge, and soon joined the staff of Ernest Rutherford, who by then was director of the Cavendish Laboratories there. Rutherford had become famous for his studies of the atom, and for a short time Appleton worked directly for him, investigating alpha particles. But Appleton's real interest was radio, and Rutherford encouraged him to pursue his own interests.

In April of 1924, Barnett came to Cambridge as Appleton's assistant. Barnett's first task was to record, as carefully as he could, the strength of the signal from a radio station the British Broadcasting Company (BBC) had opened two years before in London. He soon discovered that the strength of the signal stayed nearly constant during the daytime, but that at night its strength fluctuated up and down in an almost repetitive pattern.

Appleton had an idea why this was happening. During the day, he suggested, only one radio wave reached Cambridge from London; but during the night, two waves arrived from London. One traveled directly to Cambridge over the surface of the earth, and the other traveled upward to the atmosphere, where it was reflected back to earth. The

pattern was produced by the interference between the reflected wave and the wave traveling along the ground, as
shown in Figure 3.

The ground wave traveled by the shortest path, while
the reflected wave traveled over the longer earth-mirror-
earth path. The two waves might arrive at Oxford in step,
out of step, or somewhere in between. In the figure, A shows
the two waves arriving in step; that is, the crests of the two
waves are lined up so that added together they make the
strongest possible signal at Oxford. B shows the two waves

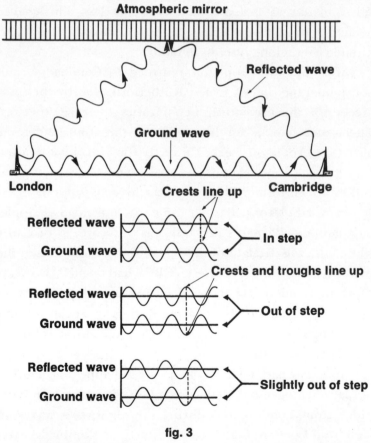

fig. 3

*Dr. Appleton's idea of two radio waves traveling from the
same transmitter*

arriving *out* of step; here the crests of one wave are opposite the troughs of the other, so that they tend to cancel each other and produce a very weak signal. C shows the in-between case, where the crests and troughs are slightly out of step; this produces a signal strength somewhere between the maximum and minimum.

The situation in C was not responsible for the fluctuating signal that Barnett observed; such a situation gives a signal of *constant* strength with the strength depending on the degree to which the two waves arrive in step. So Barnett's fluctuating signal suggested that the two waves were continually moving in and out of step. And the simplest explanation that Appleton could think of was that the atmospheric mirror must be moving up and down. As we can see from the figure, moving the mirror has no effect on the length of the ground wave, but it does change the path length for the reflected wave. So if the two waves arrived at some moment in step at Oxford, a slight upward or downward movement of the mirror would cause them to shift slightly out of step, and so reduce the signal strength.

As we said earlier, it was on the night of Marconi's address to the Royal Society of Arts that Appleton and Barnett set out for Oxford to test Appleton's theory. Appleton had arranged with the BBC to conduct a special test using the BBC station at Bournemouth, England. The tests were to be conducted around midnight of the following day. The plan was to have the station at Bournemouth slowly shift its transmitting frequency while Appleton and Barnett recorded the signal strength at Oxford. If Appleton's theory about there being two waves was correct, shifting the transmitting frequency would produce a fluctuating signal at Oxford.

Figure 4 shows the ground and reflected waves as in Figure 3. But this time as we look from left to right we see that the frequency gradually increases for both the ground and reflected waves. This represents the change in frequency of

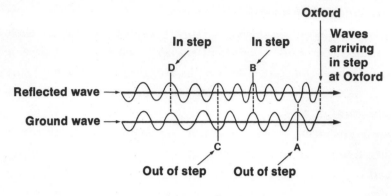

fig. 4

the signal sent from Bournemouth. At the particular instant we have chosen, the waves are arriving in step at Oxford, giving a maximum signal strength. But a few moments later, the two wave segments marked "A" arrive at Oxford. And we notice that they are out of step, so that the signal strength decreases. But after a few moments more, segment B arrives, again producing a maximum signal. Following this line of reasoning, we can see that the signal continually fluctuates in strength at Oxford as long as the transmitted frequency continues to be shifted upward or downward.

Within a few minutes after the tests were started, it was clear that Appleton's theory was working; the signal fluctuated in strength just as he had predicted. By measuring the number of fluctuations during a certain period, Appleton was also able to figure out the height of the reflecting layer; it turned out to be about 100 km.

Appleton continued his experiments and soon discovered that there was not just one but at least two reflecting layers in the atmosphere. Not knowing how many might eventually be discovered, he named the lower layer the *E region* and the upper layer the *F region*. Later another, lower layer was discovered, which was named the *D region,* in accordance with Appleton's scheme.

As Appleton and others before him suspected, the mirror in the atmosphere—today called the *ionosphere*—is due to radiation from the sun. Rutherford, we recall, discovered that atoms consist of central, compact, positively charged cores surrounded by circling electrons. High in the atmosphere, the sun's rays are at full strength and can strip electrons away from their atoms, leaving many electrons free to move about in space. We remember also that electric currents in antennas can radiate radio waves. So let's think of the free electrons in the ionosphere as miniature antennas that broadcast radio signals back to earth.

Before a radio transmitter is turned on, the free electrons move about more or less at random in the ionosphere. But when a transmitter is turned on, part of its signal moves toward the upper atmosphere, where it meets the free electrons. As we know by now, electric fields cause currents to flow; so the fluctuating electric field in the radio wave causes the free electrons to vibrate with the same frequency as the radio wave. Then these vibrating electrons, moving back and forth like currents in the antenna, radiate radio waves. The transmitted radio wave causes the electrons in the ionosphere to vibrate, and the vibrating electrons reradiate or reflect the signal back to earth.

Appleton developed a mathematical theory for this reflection process that explained why Barnett had observed two signals at night but only one during the daytime. His theory also explained Marconi's earlier observation that signals seemed to disappear over distances greater than 1,100 km during the daytime, whereas they remained quite strong at even greater distances at night.

The key to these observations is that during the daytime, when the sun is shining on the atmosphere, the sun's rays create electrons below the reflecting layer at 100 km. Here the atmosphere is very dense; so just as an electron begins to move under the influence of a radio signal, it collides with a nearby atom and gives up its energy to the atom instead. In other words, during the daytime the radio signal never reaches the reflection level, but is "absorbed" because of collisions between free electrons and the surrounding atoms. So during the daytime only the ground wave reaches the receiver. At night, however, the radio signals are not absorbed, and both the ground wave and the reflected wave reach the receiver. This explains the fluctuating pattern that Barnett observed.

The explanation of Marconi's observation is that he received mainly the ground wave during the day because the reflected wave was largely absorbed. But at night he received mainly the reflected wave, since at distances over 1,100 km the ground wave is very weak. In 1947 Appleton received a Nobel prize in physics for his discovery of the ionosphere.

The ionosphere provides an electronic mirror to return earth-launched signals to the ground, but it can also keep out or distort signals transmitted from above it toward the earth. Before the days of artificial satellites, this did not seem like a very important problem. But as we shall see later, the ionosphere causes a problem for radio signals transmitted from satellites.

III

Electronics— The Invisible Thread

12.
The Light Bulb that Grew Up to Be a Radio Tube

In Section II such names as Faraday, Crookes, Edison, Marconi, and others keep reappearing. By the end of the nineteenth century, however, a basic set of laws that govern all magnetic and electrical phenomena was beginning to emerge. What had been a hit-or-miss approach to developing new devices by scientists and nonscientists, engineers and nonengineers was now turning into a more systematic approach with specific goals. There were still surprises along the way, as there are today. But more and more, progress resulted from the work of a large group of people with strong backgrounds in science and engineering. So as we move into the further development of the vast communication web, it becomes impossible to cite every name associated with each development, or to track down the many threads that led to a particular development.

Still many of the developments in the recent past and the present are associated with particular names. One is Sir Ambrose Fleming, an English scientist who at one time worked for the Edison Company in England. Fleming was interested in improving the detection of radio signals; and the key to his system was provided unwittingly by Thomas Edison, who had invented a light bulb that used an electrically heated carbon filament to generate light. Edison noticed that over a period of time, the bulb darkened inside because of the continuous "evaporation" of carbon from the filament.

Trying to learn more about how this evaporation took place, Edison placed a small metal plate inside the bulb, as shown in Figure 1. He then noticed that when he connected

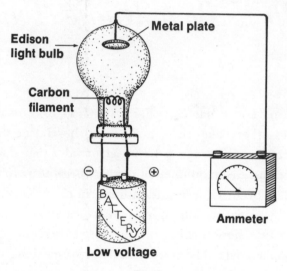

fig. 1

Edison's light bulb

the plate to the positive terminal of the battery supplying current to the filament, a small current flowed from the plate back to the battery. Since the plate stopped the darkening of the bulb Edison patented his light bulb with the plate inside, but he pursued the subject no further.

In Chapter 7 we mentioned the *coherer*—the device Marconi used to detect radio waves. The coherer consisted of a small, sealed tube of glass loosely filled with iron filings. A wire extended from each end, and these were attached to two antenna wires, as shown in Figure 2.

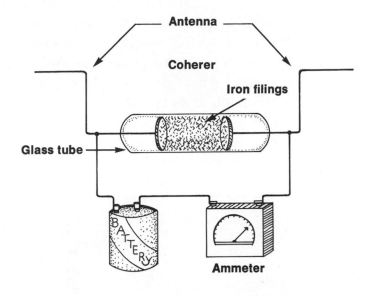

fig. 2

A "coherer" detects radio signals

As we know, an antenna in the presence of a radio wave generates an electrical signal. Workers before Marconi had discovered that such a signal caused the iron filings in the coherer to crowd so close together that a current could pass through it. Figure 2 shows the two wires protruding from the coherer also attached by wires to a battery and an ammeter. When a radio signal is present, the mechanism becomes *conducting* and allows the current from the battery to flow through the coherer, where it is detected or measured by the ammeter.

Before the radio signal arrives, the coherer is *nonconducting* so no current flows through the ammeter. One big problem with the coherer was that after it became conducting it stayed that way, even though no radio signal was present. The reason was that once the iron filings crowded together, they remained in that position until someone tapped the tube and knocked them apart. This awkward situation, plus some other difficulties with the coherer, led Fleming to look for a new kind of detector, and he suspected that the "Edison Effect" might be the clue to building a better one.

Fleming continued with Edison's experiments and discovered several interesting new effects. First, if he connected the plate in the light bulb to the positive terminal of a high-voltage battery, a large current flowed through the ammeter, as shown in Figure 3. But if he connected the negative terminal of the battery to the plate, no current flowed.

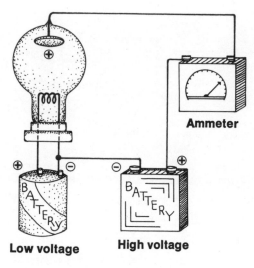

Ammeter

Low voltage   **High voltage**

fig. 3

Fleming's "diode tube" was a big improvement over the coherer

Now that we know about atoms and electrons, we can explain this result, although it was not clearly understood at the time. The hot filament of the light bulb contains many atoms, which are continually colliding with each other. Some of the collisions are so severe that electrons are knocked away from the atoms whose cores they are circling. A few of these freed electrons drift away from the filament into the surrounding space, and some of these are attracted to the plate, which has a small positive charge, and then return to the battery through the wire that connects the plate to the battery's positive terminal. This is what Edison measured.

But when Fleming connected the *positive* terminal of a high-voltage battery to the plate, the negative electrons drifting away from the filament were now attracted in large numbers to the positively charged plate. This explains the dramatic increase in the *plate current,* as it is usually called. On the other hand, when Fleming connected the *negative* terminal of the battery to the plate, the plate current stopped because the electrons drifting away from the filament were now repelled by the negatively charged plate.

Let's suppose now that we remove the battery and replace it with the current from an ordinary electrical outlet. In most parts of the United States, and in a good part of the rest of the world, the current from such an outlet is called *alternating current,* which is usually abbreviated "AC." In contrast to the *direct current,* or DC, that comes from a battery, AC flows rapidly forward and backward, first in one direction and then in the other. For example, 60-cycle AC means that the current switches direction 60 times a second.

Figure 4 illustrates AC. The graph is divided into the upper, positive half and the lower, negative half. The repeated curve represents the current flow. When the curve is in the upper, positive half, the current flows in the positive direction; and when it is in the lower half, current flows in the negative or opposite direction.

When we connect AC to the plate in the light bulb, the charge on the plate alternates back and forth between positive and negative. When the plate is positive, electrons flow from the filament to the plate; and when the plate is negative, no electrons or current flows. Figure 5 illustrates how current flows only when the plate is positive. The solid portion of the curve represents current flowing during the time

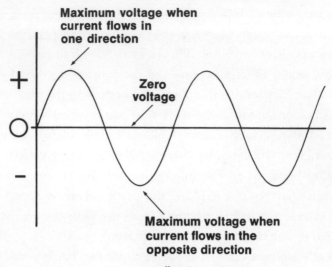

Maximum voltage when
current flows in
one direction

Zero
voltage

+

O

−

Maximum voltage when
current flows in the
opposite direction

fig. 4

Alternating current

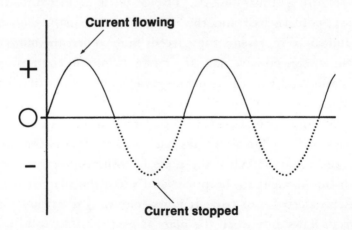

Current flowing

+

O

−

Current stopped

fig. 5

Direct current

when the plate is positive, and the broken portion represents the time when the plate is negative, with no current flowing.

So we see that the current flows intermittently, every other half cycle, in one direction only. The light bulb with a plate in it acts as a "gate" that lets current flow only in one direction. Such devices are produced by the millions today, and are called *diodes* because they have two elements: a filament and a plate.

What does this have to do with detecting radio waves? Well, as we know, radio waves are very-high-frequency signals that were first produced in a "Hertz transmitter" by a spark that jumped rapidly back and forth between the two ends of a wire loop separated by a short distance. This jumping back and forth of the spark is really nothing but an alternating current, because the current flows first one way and then the other. In a similar sense, the radio wave, when it interacts with a receiving antenna, produces a current in the antenna that flows rapidly back and forth.

If we connect the antenna signal to a meter whose pointer moves in one direction when the signal is positive and in the other when it is negative, the pointer will barely move. This is because the radio waves are at such a high frequency that the pointer just begins to move in one direction when it must reverse to indicate flow in the other direction. Because it cannot change direction fast enough, it hardly moves at all.

But suppose we take the current from our antenna and connect it to the plate of a diode: Current flows only when the antenna is positive. So now the pointer does not have to dart rapidly back and forth. It moves only when the plate of the diode is positive. Furthermore, since the pointer can't fall back to its "zero" position at the instant the radio signal goes from positive to negative, it tends to stay at one nearly fixed position as long as a radio signal is present.

The Fleming diode was a huge improvement over the coherer for detecting radio waves, but there was still the problem that radio signals are very weak and some method was needed to amplify them. An American scientist and inventor, Lee De Forest, tackled this problem. His solution was based on a relatively minor but important modification of the Fleming diode. He introduced a wire mesh, today called a *grid,* between the filament and the plate.

When there is no charge on the grid, electrons from the filament pass easily through the mesh on their way to the plate. But when the grid is negative, it repels the electrons and keeps them from getting through to the plate. The more negative the grid, the slower the flow of electrons between filament and plate. We might think of the grid as a sort of Venetian blind; just a slight adjustment of the blind causes a large change in the amount of light passing through. In just such a way, a very small fluctuating signal on the grid controls the much more powerful current that flows between the filament and the plate.

Let's suppose, for example, that we "feed" the signal from one of Edison's carbon microphones to the grid, as shown in Figure 6. As we speak into the microphone it creates a tiny current that changes the charge on the grid. These small changes in charge produce big changes in the plate current flowing in the tube. Then if we connect the plate current to a loudspeaker, the sound produced by the loudspeaker will be much stronger than the sound of our voice at the microphone.

This tube is called a *triode* because it has three elements—filament, plate, and grid. It can be used to amplify any kind of radio or electrical signal as well as sound signals. De Forest first offered his tube to the telephone companies to amplify their phone signals, and eventually such tubes were used by the thousands for this purpose. Develop-

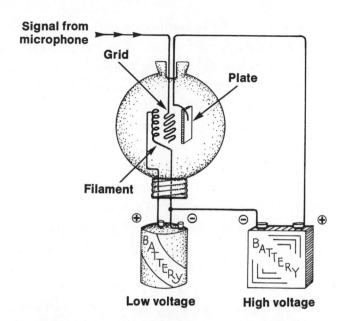

Signal from microphone

Grid

Plate

Filament

⊕ ⊖

Low voltage

⊖ ⊕

High voltage

fig. 6 DEFOREST'S TRIODE RADIO TUBE

ment of the triode and related amplifying devices made it possible to send telephone calls along transoceanic cables.

The De Forest triode also solved another problem. As we know, the Hertz transmitter generated signals over a wide range of frequencies, and this created severe interference problems between stations. De Forest found that if he took a small portion of the signal that came from the plate and "fed it back" to the grid, he could generate signals at a single frequency.

Perhaps you have observed a variation of this principle in an auditorium when the sound system emits a loud, screeching noise. What happens is that as the speaker talks into the microphone, the loudspeakers produce an amplified version of his voice. If the system is turned up too much, part of the amplified sound makes its way back to the microphone. Then the system is amplifying not only the speaker's voice, but also the sound from its own loudspeakers. This combination increases the volume of sound from the loudspeakers, which in turn again increases the sound level at the microphone. Finally the system becomes overloaded by its own sound and breaks into a piercing screech.

In a similar way, the grid in a vacuum tube corresponds to the microphone; and if part of the signal from the plate that corresponds to the loudspeakers finds its way back to the grid, then the triode tube also goes into a "screeching mode." But in this case the screeching mode is just what we want because it corresponds to producing a signal at a single frequency. The kinds of electrical circuits where *feedback* is employed in conjunction with triodes are called *oscillator circuits* because they vibrate or oscillate at a particular frequency. Later we shall learn how diode and triode radio tubes have been replaced by newer devices that perform the same functions.

13.
Voices & Music Through the Air

Wires and cables carry messages along specific routes to specific destinations. Until Bell and others developed mechanisms that made it possible for voice communication by telephone, the messages were limited to dots and dashes that could be understood only by operators with special training.

Radio signals travel in all directions from a transmitter, and can be "tuned in" by anyone with the necessary receiver within range of the signal. At first radio messages, too, were limited to dots and dashes; but people soon began to wonder about the possibilities of talking directly through the air.

There is one big difference between telephone and radio signals, however: Telephone signals are just "electrical mimics" of the sound signals generated by devices like Edison's carbon microphone. The 1,000-cycle-per-second note produced by someone singing or whistling the note over the telephone is turned into a 1,000-cycle-per-second electrical signal, which in turn is converted back to the original sound signal at the listener's earpiece.

But the radio signals used by Marconi in his early broadcasts—like those used today—were at many tens of thousands of cycles per second, well above the highest frequency that the human ear can detect. The trick, then, seemed to be somehow to use the high-frequency radio signals to "carry" in some "piggyback" fashion the lower-frequency signals making up the human voice.

The problem was first solved by Reginald A. Fessenden, a Canadian teacher turned inventor. Fessenden realized that radio signals could be made to carry the human voice if some means could be found to generate a "pure" radio signal—a signal at a single frequency.

Fessenden left Canada for the United States to work for the Edison Machine Works, where by age 22 he was chief chemist; but he was keenly interested in wireless voice transmissions, and left Edison's company in 1899 to pursue this interest. By December of 1900, he had succeeded in transmitting wireless speech.

The first problem Fessenden faced was to replace the Hertz spark transmitter with some other device. We recall that the Hertz transmitter generated a wide range of frequencies, and what Fessenden wanted was a device that created only one radio frequency. We have just learned how this was achieved by using the triode invented by De Forest. But Fessenden's search took place more than a decade before the triode oscillator was developed.

His solution was to build an electric generator, much like the generators in today's electric power stations except that his generator created electrical signals at many thousands of cycles per second, instead of the 60-cycle-per-second currents we receive from the power stations.

Figure 1-a illustrates the radio signal generated by Fessenden's generator. The frequency of this particular signal is 10,000 cycles per second, which means that each cycle repeats itself 10,000 times every second. Below the radio signal, in Figure 1-b, we also illustrate the 1,000-cycle-per-second signal produced by the person singing or whistling the note.

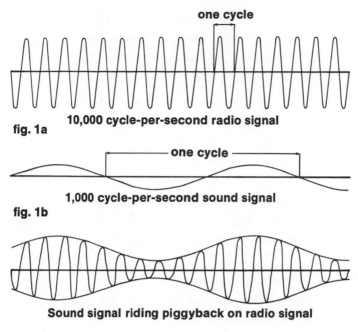

one cycle

10,000 cycle-per-second radio signal

fig. 1a

one cycle

1,000 cycle-per-second sound signal

fig. 1b

Sound signal riding piggyback on radio signal

fig. 1c

What Fessenden did was to "impress" this sound on the radio signal. This combination of sound-radio signal is shown in Figure 1-c. Here we see the original high-frequency radio signal fluctuating in strength, or *amplitude,* at the rate of 1,000 times per second; this is what a radio signal "carrying" a 1,000-cycle-per-second sound signal looks like.

At the radio receiver, the low-frequency sound signal is separated from the high-frequency radio signal. The sound signal is then amplified and fed into the speaker of a radio to reproduce the original singing sound. Impressing the sound signal on the radio signal is called *modulation,* and this particular kind of modulation is called *amplitude modulation* (AM) because the strength, or amplitude, of the radio signal, which at first is steady as shown in Figure 1-a, is modulated by the sound signal—or the *modulating signal,* as it is usually called.

At radio broadcasting stations the signal that modulates

the radio signal is produced by someone speaking into a microphone. This signal is then combined with the radio signal in a device called a *modulator,* which produces the signal shown in Figure 1-c.

Of course, the human speaking voice is much more complicated than just a simple singing or whistling tone. It consists of a combination of many sound frequencies ranging from less than a hundred to several thousand cycles per second. This means that the voice signal that is modulated onto the radio signal—or *carrier signal,* as it is usually called—is more complicated than the simple 1,000-cycle-per-second signal we have shown. But the principle is the same. By 1906, Fessenden had improved his system to the point where he could broadcast both voice and music with considerable clarity. On Christmas eve of that year, he broadcast a signal from the Massachusetts coast which was picked up by many startled radio operators on ships along the Atlantic coast who were used to hearing only the dots and dashes of radio-telegraphy signals along with the usual background static. That night they heard a man giving a speech, a woman singing, and the mellow strains of a violin.

It was another 14 years before the first United States commercial radio broadcast, from a station in Pittsburg. Improvements during these years included replacement of Fessenden's generator with the more compact, less expensive, all electronic oscillator circuits. But even today, AM radio is based upon the system developed by Fessenden.

If you have ever listened to AM radio when the signal is weak or during a thunderstorm, you know that static can sometimes completely drown out the program. In the early days of radio, technicians thought that the best way to reduce static was to tune the radio receiver as nearly as possible to the station signal. What does this mean? Well, if we look at the dots and dashes of a radio-telegraphy signal, we see short and long bursts of the radio signal. All of these are at the same frequency—the frequency of the radio signal. So the best kind of receiver for radio-telegraphy signals is one that lets in just the radio frequency associated with the bursts, and no others. If the receiver lets in other frequencies, the wireless operator may hear other, interfering stations, plus any "noise," such as lightning flashes, present at these other frequencies.

Let's suppose now that we tune a radio-telegraphy kind of receiver—one that lets in just a single frequency—to an AM signal of the kind shown in Figure 1-c. What will we hear? Nothing, or practically nothing. As we know, this signal is a combination of the original radio signal at 10,000 cycles per second and the modulation signal at 1,000 cycles per second. It seems clear that our AM signal is something more than just a signal at 50,000 cycles per second, and to tune to just that single frequency will exclude the modulation signal.

How, then, can we tune in this signal? Well, our AM radio receiver must let in a "band" of frequencies wide enough to include both the 50,000-cycle-per-second carrier frequency and the modulation signal. Since the modulation signal is at 1,000 cycles per second, the AM receiver must let in a band of frequencies from 50,000 plus 1,000 to 50,000 minus 1,000 cycles per second, as shown in Figure 2. Or, as

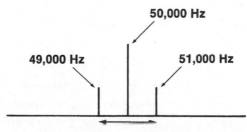

**The AM receiver must let in frequencies
over this band width**

fig. 2

it is usually said, the *bandwidth* of the receiver has to be 2,000 Hertz (Hz)—ranging from 49,000 to 51,000 Hz. Hertz is the term scientists use to mean cycles per second, and we shall use it from now on; the name comes, of course, from the discoverer of radio waves, Heinrich Hertz.

Why is the bandwidth of the receiver twice as wide as the modulation frequency? The answer has to do with the way the modulator at the transmitter works. This kind of modulator, called a *double sideband modulator,* puts the modulation signal at both above and below the carrier frequency—that is, at both 49,000 Hz and 51,000 Hz. So in a sense the modulation is being sent twice—hence the term "double sideband." The modulation signal is in a band of frequencies on both sides of the carrier signal at 50,000 Hz. Another, newer kind of system called "single sideband" requires a bandwidth just equal to the modulating frequency. With this system a musical note at 2,000 Hz requires only a 2,000 Hz bandwidth.

AM radio stations in the United States have transmission bandwidths 10,000 Hz wide. This means that they can send modulation frequencies up to 5,000 Hz, which is sufficient for reasonable clarity of the human voice. AM radio receivers, then, should let in only a bandwidth of frequencies 10,000 Hz wide. A wider frequency will let in unnecessary signals, and a smaller one will cut out some of the modulation frequencies.

One way to increase the fidelity of a broadcast signal is to increase the bandwidth. The sounds generated by a symphony orchestra go well above 5,000 Hz; to restrict AM radio to a 10,000-Hz bandwidth obviously cuts out the sounds above 5,000 Hz, and we simply do not hear these. So why not simply increase the bandwidth? First, because the wider the bandwidth of each AM radio station, the less room there is for other stations within the band of frequencies reserved for AM radio. Second, as we increase the bandwidth of the transmitted signal, we must also increase the bandwidth of the receiver. But as we know, increasing the receiver bandwidth lets in more noise.

So we have a problem. To increase the fidelity, we must increase the bandwidth, but this requires letting in more noise at the receiver. Although many scientists thought the problem unsolvable, an American engineer, Edwin Howard Armstrong, came up with an answer in 1933.

As a child Armstrong had been impressed with Marconi's experiments. After finishing high school he decided to study electrical engineering at Columbia University, in New York, where he became interested in the "radio static problem." His professor was not optimistic about a solution. "God gave man radio," he said, "and the devil made static."

But Armstrong persisted. He was convinced that the fidelity of radio could be improved by increasing the transmission bandwidth in spite of the fact that more noise would be let in at the receiver. Armstrong's idea was to *frequency modulate* the carrier, instead of the amplitude modulation that Fessenden had used.

To understand frequency modulation, let's return to our singer at the microphone. Suppose she sings a note at just one frequency—say 1,000 Hz, and that she starts off by singing very softly and gradually increases the loudness. In frequency modulation, or FM systems, a device called an FM modulator causes the frequency of the carrier frequency to change, as shown in Figure 3. We see that as the tone goes from its minimum to its maximum volume, the carrier frequency goes from 50,000 Hz to 60,000 Hz. The *amount* by which the carrier frequency changes can be made any amount we like; it just depends on how we adjust the FM modulator at the station. For example, we could readjust the modulator so that the same variation in tone strength caused the carrier frequency to go from 50,000 to 100,000 Hz.

We see, then, how a sound signal can "spread" the car-

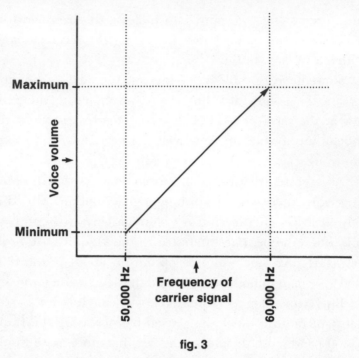

fig. 3

*In FM radio, the frequency of the carrier signal increases
with the volume of the voice signal*

rier signal as much as we like. In a similar way, a change in
frequency of the sound signal can cause the frequency of the
carrier signal to change by any amount we please. And this
is how Armstrong, using FM, could take a sound signal and
spread it over a much wider range of frequencies than the
sound signal originally occupied.

On the other hand, of course, the bandwidth of the FM
receiver must be wide enough to accept the spread-out signal.
This seems to bring up back to our original problem: We
only let in more noise by increasing the receiver bandwidth. How does FM avoid this problem?

For several years Armstrong had a continuing argument
with a number of "experts" who had analyzed FM and said
it wouldn't work. Finally, in 1933, Armstrong demonstrated

before a dumbfounded group of listeners that FM radio could provide nearly static-free reception.

One of the reasons for the controversy was that the mathematical analysis of FM radio is rather complicated, and it was not easy to see where the improvement came from. Although we cannot go into the mathematics here, we can consider a simple illustration that suggests how FM radio works.

Suppose we want to send a letter to a friend. Normally, we write the letter, put it in an envelope, and mail it. Let's suppose, however, that our letter gets mangled in the processing machine at the Post Office, and the message in our letter is destroyed. In a similar sense, when we are listening to an AM broadcast, a nearby lightning flash can create a burst of noise that momentarily destroys what is being said.

Let's suppose now that the message we wish to send to our friend is very important, and we don't want anything to happen to it. So we think of a scheme. We put each word of the message in a different envelope. That is, we "spread out" the message by sending many letters instead of just one. It's not likely that *all* of the envelopes will be mangled; most should arrive with no difficulty. After our friend has received the letters, he can reassemble the message. We might say, then, that the message was spread out to protect it, and at the receiving end it is "de-spread" to obtain the message.

In a similar way in FM radio, the signal is spread out in frequency at the transmitter, and at the receiver it is "de-spread" to obtain the original signal. This spreading in frequency helps protect the signal from noise caused by lightning or any other kind of electrical noise. We shall return to this "spreading" idea in the next chapter.

By 1939, 150 companies had applied for FM licenses; but then two things happened that greatly slowed the development of FM radio: The world became embroiled in World War II, and a competitor—television—appeared on the scene.

Today TV and FM radio thrive together; but in the days when they were both emerging, many were afraid that two new communication technologies could not be introduced successfully at the same time. So TV was given the go-ahead. But after TV was firmly established, FM radio began to grow again.

14.
Painting Pictures with Electrons

Hundreds of engineers and scientists have contributed to the development of television as we know it today. But before TV became a practical reality, many schemes—some silly, some amazingly close to TV as it now operates—were considered. We won't recount all of these schemes here, but a few of them anticipated some of the principles necessary to understanding how TV works; so we shall describe these briefly.

As early as 1875, a Bostonian named George R. Carey proposed a TV system that resembled the human eye. The main component of Carey's system was an element called selenium. An important part in most electrical systems is called a *resistor;* as the name suggests, a resistor "resists" the flow of electricity, and selenium is a substance that has this property. A telegraph operator in Ireland had noticed that the selenium resistors at his station were sensitive to light. The brighter the light shone on the selenium, the lower its resistance to electric current flow. This chance discovery inspired Carey to propose a system that would "electrically transmit silhouettes."

Figure 1-a shows a selenium cell connected to a battery and an ammeter. A current flows through the cell when it is

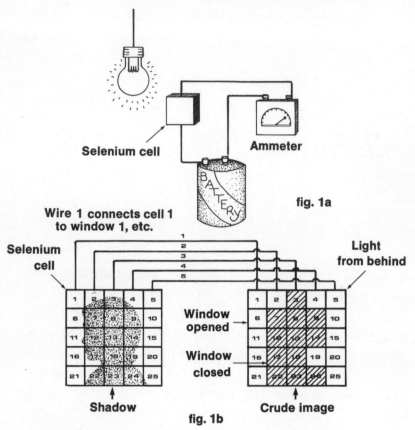

Wire 1 connects cell 1 to window 1, etc.

Selenium cell

Ammeter

fig. 1a

Selenium cell

Light from behind

Window opened →

Window closed →

Shadow

Crude image

fig. 1b

Light shining on selenium cells transmits a crude silhouette

exposed to light. Carey imagined that a number of these cells arranged in a grid system, as in Figure 1-b, could be used to transmit a silhouette. Each of the cells in the grid is connected by a wire to a cell in a similar grid system at the viewer's end. The cells at the viewer's end are "windows" that open and close by electromagnets, depending on whether or not a current is flowing in the wire connecting the selenium cell to its corresponding window.

A person standing in front of the transmitting grid will cast a shadow on it. The selenium cells in the shadow area will not conduct a current to operate the electro-magnets at the viewer's end; so those windows will remain closed. But the selenium cells not in the shadow will conduct a current to open the windows, letting light shine through from a lamp placed behind the viewer's grid. So the viewer will see an image of the shadow cast on the transmitting grid. If the shadow at the transmitting grid moves, so will the image at the receiving grid.

One thing that determines the quality or *image fidelity* of this system is the size and number of the cells. If the cells are large and few, the image will be crude and coarse like the one in the figure. But if the cells are small and numerous, the image will resemble the shadow quite accurately. This is still an important principle in television today. As we shall see, the TV image is divided into many *picture elements,* and as with Carey's system, the greater the number of picture elements, the better the TV image.

One big problem with Carey's proposal is that each selenium cell must be connected by a wire to its corresponding window. This reminds us of Ampère's telegraph system, in which each letter of the alphabet required its own wire. And as with Ampère's system, Carey's system would be very cumbersome and expensive to build because of the many wires. The solution for television, then, is similar to the one eventually adopted for the telegraph—sending the TV image one picture element at a time, over a single wire or a single *channel.*

This solution occurred to a French lawyer, Constantin Senlecq, in 1877. Figure 2 shows his system. The image to be transmitted is projected onto a partially transparent screen. Behind the screen is a pointer connected to a horizontal and a vertical arm so that the pointer can be moved to any location behind the screen. The operation of this device is much the same as the familiar "Etch-a-Sketch" which you have probably used to create your own drawings by turning two knobs at the bottom of a screen.

Let's suppose again that a person's shadow is cast on the

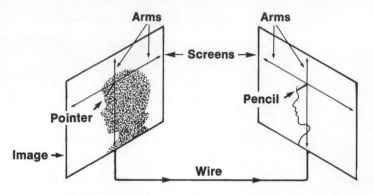

Two systems connected by a single wire that carries "location information"

fig. 2

screen. We trace the pointer around the edge of the shadow. The pointer arrangement is connected by a wire to a similar arm arrangement at the viewer's end. But here the pointer is replaced by a pencil that draws on the screen. A signal that indicates the location of the pointer flows through the wire and causes the pencil to move in step with the pointer.

This system requires someone to move the pointer around the edge of the shadow; an automatic system would be better. So suppose we move the pointer to the upper left-hand corner of the screen and let it *scan* the shadow from left to right across the screen, as shown in Figure 3-a. When the pointer reaches the right-hand edge of the screen, it automatically moves rapidly back to the left edge and scans across again, a little below its original path—in much the same pattern you use in reading this page. If this process is repeated many times, as shown in Figure 3-b, the pointer scans the whole screen, line by line, ending with line 50. A similar scanning system was used to send *facsimile* photographs by telephone to newspapers long before it was adapted for TV.

What signal travels along the wire in this system? If the pointer could talk, it might give instructions to the pencil something like this:

Pointer   **Pencil**

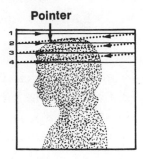 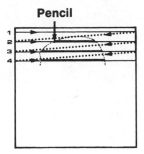

fig. 3a

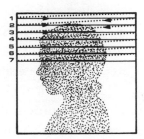 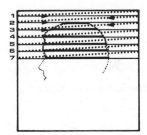

fig. 3b

1. I am at the left edge of the screen at line 1;
   move to that position.
2. I am moving across line 1 now, and when I
   come to the shadow I will tell you to start tracing a line.
3. I am at the edge of the shadow now. Start tracing and continue until I tell you to stop.
4. I have reached the right edge of the shadow;
   stop tracing and continue until I tell you I have
   reached the right edge of the screen.
5. I have reached the right edge. Move back to the
   beginning of line 2.

If this series of instructions is carried out, over and over
again until the pointer reaches line 50, an image of the
shadow will be drawn at the viewer's screen, as shown in

Figure 4. If the image consisted of 500 horizontal lines instead of 50, the picture quality would be better.

Although the details are somewhat different, modern television works this way. At the sending end, the electronic "pointer" scans the image, and at the viewer's end, an electronic "pencil" draws the picture. Obviously, the pencil must always be exactly in step, or in *synchronization,* with the pointer. *Scanning* and *synchronization* are two key elements in television transmission and reception.

The first practical television system started operation in 1926. It had all of the elements we have discussed: scanning, synchronization, and picture fidelity—or *resolution,* as it is usually called—which depends on the number of picture elements or scanning lines. The system did not operate exactly as we've described it, however, for it still had a number of mechanical parts that limited its resolution. Many technicians realized that an all-electronic system, with no moving parts, would be far better.

The key to such a system was a development we'll recognize from our discussion of the discovery of the electron.

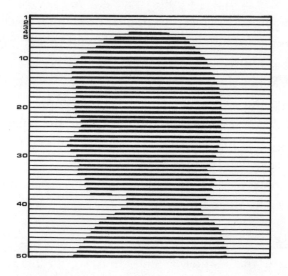

fig. 4

We recall that some of the properties of electrons were determined by observing how cathode rays, which are simply
streams of electrons, are deflected in evacuated glass tubes by
electric and magnetic fields. It seemed reasonable, then, that
it would be possible to use a "pencillike" beam of electrons,
in an evacuated tube, to "draw" an image. The electron
beam would be directed by electric and magnetic fields.

One problem was how to make the path taken by the
electrons visible. A German scientist, Karl Ferdinand Braun,
provided the answer in 1897. He invented a *cathode ray* tube
with a *fluorescent* screen; fluorescent screens produce light
when struck by electrons.

Braun's tube is shown in Figure 5. At the narrow end is a
cathode which emits electrons. The electrons are attracted to
the positive electrode, called the *anode*. But some of the electrons "slide by" the anode and hit the fluorescent screen at
the wide end of the tube.

If a beam of electrons in the tube is directed, for example, to move in a circle, a dot of light moves in a circle on the
screen. If the electrons trace out the circle very rapidly, it

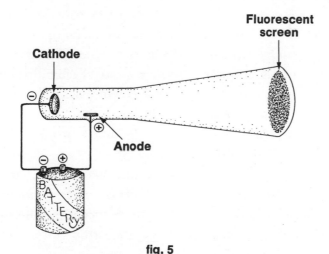

fig. 5
Braun's cathode ray tube had no moving parts

will appear to the human eye that a complete circle is momentarily in view. The effect is similar to that of someone waving a flashlight in front of you on a dark night. If he swings the flashlight rapidly in a circle, it appears to your eye that a circle is drawn out in the air, while in fact, there is only a spot of light moving in a circle.

This phenomenon is called *persistence of vision,* and it means simply that the eye tends to "smear out" the image of a rapidly moving object. As we shall see, it is this characteristic of the human visual system that makes it possible to transmit an image, picture element by picture element, instead of "all at once" as in Carey's many-wire system.

The first practical all-electronic TV picture tube was built in 1929 by Vladimir Zworykin, who came to the United States from Russia in 1919. It was also Zworykin who, in 1931, built the first practical all-electronic TV camera. Both were based on the idea of steering electron beams in a cathode-ray tube. The steering can be done by either electric or magnetic fields, or some combination of these fields.

Figure 6 shows a TV picture tube in which the electron beam is steered by magnetic fields. The fields are produced by currents flowing in two coils of wires contained in the *deflection yoke.* The coils can move the beam up and down and back and forth across the screen. The TV signal contains instructions similar to those we listed earlier, to control the currents in the deflection yoke. The changing currents in the deflection yoke cause the beam to scan back and forth across the screen in step with the "pointer" in the TV camera, "painting" the picture in electrons.

The TV signal also contains information that controls the flow of electrons from the cathode or *electron gun,* as we have labeled it in the figure. When the "scene" at the studio is bright, the TV signal instructs the electron gun to step up its electron emission so that more electrons hit the screen and cause it to brighten.

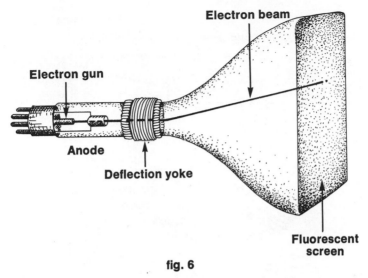

fig. 6

Zworykin's TV picture tube

Although a TV camera is somewhat more complicated than a receiver, it is in a way just the reverse of the receiver. A TV camera converts the image in front of it into an electrical signal, and a TV receiver converts the electrical signal back into an image.

Figure 7 is a sketch of Zworykin's first camera, which he called an "iconoscope." Light from the televised scene is focused by the *focusing lens* onto a special screen at the back of the camera. The front of the screen is called the *mosaic,* and just behind it is a sheet of mica that electrically insulates the mosaic from a metal plate called the *signal plate*.

If we looked at the mosaic under a microscope, we would see that it is covered with thousands of tiny silver beads coated with another metal, *cesium.* We would also notice that no two beads touch each other; each stands alone from all the others. When light strikes these beads, they give off electrons. If bright light falls on a particular bead, it gives off many electrons; if the light is dimmer, it gives off fewer electrons. That is, the beads in the brighter areas of the im-

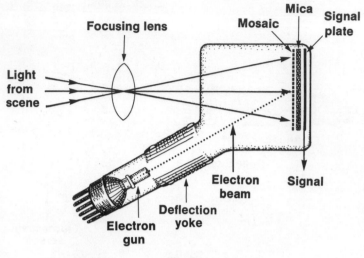

fig. 7

Zworykin's TV camera

age have a greater positive charge than do those in areas where the light is weaker. In this way the scene is reproduced on the mosaic by thousands of beads with different amounts of positive charge. This is the first step toward changing the image to an electrical signal.

The next step is to measure the variation in positive electric charge on the beads and convert this variation into an electrical signal. To do this an electron beam scans the beads left to right and top to bottom, just as in the TV picture tube. In the United States there are 525 scanning lines, which gives enough resolution for most purposes. It takes only 1/30 second to scan the complete image. Or put differently, the electron beam scans the image 30 times every second.

As the electron beam scans a particular line of beads, it comes upon beads with varying positive charge and "gives up" electrons to replace the ones driven off by the light. So the number of electrons flowing in the electron beam fluctuates up and down as it encounters beads with more or less positive charge.

The beads going from positive back to neutral causes an electric current to flow from the signal plate behind the mica insulator. The amount of current generated in the signal plate at a particular instant depends on the number of electrons being given off by the electron beam. So we have now achieved our goal of converting the visual image into an electrical signal, 525 lines long.

A single line of electrical signal follows the brightness of the part of the image scanned. It is the TV receiver's job, then, to reassemble these lines at the viewer's end to form the image.

To make sure that the lines at the receiver are electronically painted in step with the lines generated by the TV camera, an extra piece of information is added to each line by the camera. These *synchronization pulses* tell the receiver how to reassemble the lines correctly.

As we watch a TV program, it appears to our eyes that the motion is continuous. But as we now know, the picture is really just a series of pictures—30 per second—each composed of a large number of variously lighted horizontal lines. It is only because of the "persistence of vision" that the TV picture seems to be smooth and continuous.

A big improvement in television came with the introduction of color. Although this was technically a very difficult problem, the principle behind it is easy to understand. You have doubtless learned in art classes at school how a particular color can be made from a combination of other colors. Red and blue mixed together, for example, make purple. This is how color TV works—and color TV has the advantage of being able to "subtract" color from a mixture, something that's impossible in mixing paints.

The studio camera separates the image before it into red, green, and blue. It then recombines these three "color images" in just the right proportions to produce a "white" signal that ordinary *black-and-white* sets can receive. This is called the "Y" signal. The camera also combines the three color images in other proportions to form two more signals— the "Q" and "I" signals. A *color* TV receiver responds to all three—the Y, Q, and I signals—to produce a color picture.

The inside of the face of a color TV picture tube is covered with thousands of phosphorescent dots; some glow red, some green, and some blue when struck by electrons. There are three electron beams in the picture tube—one for each color. The beams recreate the picture on the face of the tube by lighting up just the proper combination of phosphorescent dots.

The sound part of a TV program is almost free of static. Like FM radio, it travels by frequency modulation. The picture signal, however, is AM. Television technology is now on the verge of a new system in which both sound and pictures travel by *digital* signals. Digital TV opens a whole new array of possibilities which we shall explore in later chapters.

15.
Signal Space & Dr. Seuss

FM radio was a big improvement over AM because FM is freer from static or "noise." But there are many communication needs in which even the small amount of noise associated with FM signals is too much. The digital signals we have just mentioned have made today's emerging telephone system possible and are basic to advanced communication satellites.

The principles of digital signals will be easier to understand if we first look at how "noise" in everyday printed messages can affect their meaning. You've probably laughed at sentences or headlines in which just one letter inadvertently replaced the right one:

Special sale of bicycle fires.
Derailed brain crushes railroad depot.
The child gave his mother a kiss and a big bug.
The game warden arrested the man for coaching
    alligators.

The possibilities for errors in which wrong, transposed, or omitted letters can still result in a message that makes sense are determined by the words or "building blocks" of a language and the rules of grammar that govern the kinds of sentence structure allowed.

Although most letter scramblings result only in gibberish, it's a curious fact that the English language is more prone to errors of this kind than are other languages. This is so partly because English has an amazing number of three-letter words, and because the nouns seldom have inflection, or a change in form showing whether they are subjects or objects in sentences. The words *bat, cat, rat, fat, hat, mat, pat, sat,* and *vat* are all alike in structure except for the first letter, but of course have very different meanings; and words like *bat, cat, rat,* and *hat* remain the same whether they are grammatically subjects or objects.

We can write a simple sentence of three-letter words several different ways and still make sense: *The rat ate the bat* is an acceptable sentence. A different word order, although the message is improbable, also makes sense: *The bat ate the rat.* We could even say, with a less common structure, *The bat the rat ate;* "inversions" of this kind are sometimes used by poets. But other combinations of the words in our simple sentence don't make sense: *The bat rat the ate,* or *The ate rat bat the,* for example.

In many cases a person familiar with the language instantly recognizes the error, corrects it in thought, and goes on. But if the sentence says, *The rat ate the sat,* we know there's an error but we cannot be sure what the rat ate. It could be the *hat,* the *cat,* the *fat,* the *bat,* or even the *salt* or the *seat.* When a message consists of strings of numbers or digits, errors of this kind are very hard to detect because numbers by themselves are meaningless.

For efficient communication, we wish to pack the greatest possible amount of information into the fewest number of words. And the shorter the words, the better. But we also wish to keep possibilities of errors to a minimum, and to be able to spot errors that do occur.

With these ideas in mind, let's think about a very simple language, which we'll call the "zero-one" language. There are only two words in this language, which is the heart of digital signals—"o" and "1." And for the present discussion, we'll say that the language is governed by just two simple rules: Each sentence consists of exactly three words—no more, no less. And any combination of words can appear in a sentence. With these two words and two rules, there are eight possible sentences or *digital signals,* since the sentences are represented by combinations of the two digits o and 1.

000	101
001	100
011	110
111	010

We can "map" these signals onto the eight corners of an imaginary cube, thus giving each one a place in a kind of *signal space,* as shown in Figure 1. We put ooo at one corner, oo1 at another, and so on. Up to now we have not assigned any particular meaning to our signals; so let's do that now:

ooo – Stay where you are.
100 – Move to the east.
o1o – Move to the north.
1 1o – Move to the northeast.

oo1 – Move up.
1o1 – Move up and to the east.
o11 – Move up and to the north.
111 – Move up and to the northeast.

Suppose we wish to send a message ooo (Stay where you are.) but because of noise in our transmission system the first o is changed to a 1, so that the signal received is 100, which means "Move to the east." Such a signal error could have catastrophic consequences for a helicopter operating in a war zone. Although it is less likely, we might have *two* errors, so that ooo becomes 1 1o—"Move to the northeast." The

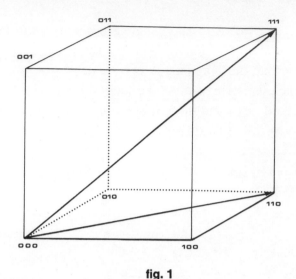

fig. 1

Each message has its own location in space

fact that two errors are less likely than one error is represented on our cube by the fact that the corner 000 is closer to the 100 corner than it is to the 110 corner. Least likely is three errors caused by noise. For example, 000 is not likely to become 111, since the corner 111 is the greatest possible distance from the corner 000.

The price we have paid for assigning meanings to every possible combination is that when there is a noise-producing error, the signal still has meaning. We have a very efficient system because every possible combination conveys information. But unless we are sure that our transmission system is noise free, we may not be able to tolerate such an efficient system. And in the "real world" of electronic communication there is no such thing as a noise-free transmission system. Sooner or later some noise will garble our messages.

Perhaps we can get by with an occasional error, and perhaps some errors have less serious consequences than others. To return to our helicopter example, the instruction 000 (Stay where you are.) may have more disastrous consequences when changed to 001 (Move up.) than any other change. In this case we would be wise to assign 111 to the message "Move up," since 111 is the greatest possible distance from 000.

In some situations it might not be necessary to assign meanings to all eight signals. The message "Move up," for example, is not meaningful when it is directed to an aircraft carrier. In fact, all messages corresponding to the top four corners of the cube have no meaning for a vessel or vehicle restricted to moving only on the surface of the land or sea. In a situation like this, we have some way to spot errors, since some sentences are not meaningful; and furthermore, confusion between messages that would lead to the most disastrous consequences can be the most widely separated. Of course, we could also assign other meanings to the top four corners of the cube when they are not needed for direction instructions. We might have for example:

> 001 – Return home
> 101 – Check fuel supply
> 011 – Check weather report
> 111 – Enemy ahead

We have noted that the density of three-letter words in the English language that helps to make it relatively efficient also makes it prone to errors. And these errors are serious because they may still result in a message that makes sense. The situation is similar to assigning meanings to all of the corners of our language cube. In fact, we might imagine a much more complex "cube" or *language space* where each word in the English language is given a particular location. Words like *cad, dad, pad, wad, gad, mad, had, bad, sad, fad,* and *lad* would be close neighbors in this language space; and words like *lad* and *hamburger* would be far apart, since there is little likelihood that noise could ever change the word *lad* into the word *hamburger,* or vice versa. It is important that words with opposite meanings not be near each other in language space. We would not like the word *yes* to sound like the word *no*. Such confusion could lead to chaos. In fact, in every spoken language words like *yes-no, up-down, black-white, stop-go* naturally separated themselves into different corners of language space.

Different languages would occupy different parts of the universe in our language space. A very efficient language would have all of its words packed in one corner of its galaxy, and a very inefficient language would have its words scattered at random over the widest possible volume. Some words would stray out into the territory of other languages.

A sentence or a string of sentences might be visualized as a snakelike line connecting the locations of the words making up the sentences. The line in its twisting, curving path will pass through some points many times because some words such as *I, a, the, and,* and *to* occur frequently. A word like *the* would be like a point on a road map where many streets come together toward the center of a city.

A Dr. Seuss story such as *Hop on Pop* or *The Cat in the Hat,* with their concentrations of short, look-alike words, would appear as a tightly wound ball of yarn. The windings of thread would lie very close together for *quick, trick,* and *sick,* and for *down* and *clown* in just one small bit of Dr. Seuss's *The Foot Book:* "Slow feet, Quick feet, Trick feet, Sick feet/Up feet, Down feet, Here come clown feet." The yarn would cross the word *feet* seven times in this brief passage.

A politician's speech or a college textbook, by contrast, would be like thin filaments of thread wandering throughout the galaxy of a language space. Sometimes it would reach out into the galaxy of another language to include a foreign word or phrase.

We might think of language space as a kind of road map of language, where dead-end roads are meaningless sentences, and where roads that connect cities and towns to one another correspond to sentences that have meaning.

Let's see now how we can apply this idea of language or *signal* space to AM and FM signals. First we recall that FM signals are more resistant to noise than AM signals. We also recall that the bandwidth occupied by our singer, singing a 1,000 Hz note, was 2,000 Hz for an AM signal; but with an FM signal, the 1,000 Hz note could be spread out to occupy any bandwidth we wish—say 10,000 Hz.

Going from AM to FM, then, is like going from a very efficient language in which every combination of letters has a meaning to a less efficient language in which some combinations have no meaning. In AM, all the information must be packed into a bandwidth that is twice the signal modulation frequency, whereas in FM the modulation signal, carrying exactly the same information as in the AM message, can be spread out as much as we like. So for FM the information is much less densely packed in signal space than it is in AM. This is a big advantage because it means that a small amount of noise that might move the message from one point in signal space to another is less likely to cause trouble in the low-density "soup" of FM signals filling the atmosphere than it is in the high-density "soup" of AM signals.

We can apply similar reasoning to digital signals made from 0's and 1's. Returning to our helicopter example, we recall that 000 meant "Stay where you are," and 001 meant "Move up." We decided that it would be better to assign the message "Move up" to 111, since the distance across the cube between 000 and 111 is greater than the distance between 000 and 001. Or stated differently, 000 is less likely to be altered by noise to 111 than to 001. Again by spreading the two messages apart in signal space we have lessened the possibility of noise transforming one message into another.

There's also another way we can minimize noise. Suppose we let 00000 mean "Stay where you are," and 00001 mean "Move up." The possibility of 00000 being changed by noise into 00001 is much less likely than 000 being changed to 001. Once more by letting each of the messages individually occupy a greater volume of signal space, we have reduced the possibility for error.

We see, then, that by spreading out a digital message sufficiently far in signal space, we can reduce the effects of noise as much as we like. The only practical limitation is that the amount of signal space available to us may be limited, just as AM radio stations are limited to 10 kHz bandwidths.

An understanding of signal space helps us to design secret messages so that they will not be intercepted by outsiders who may tune in on them. Or to insure that a signal arrives at its intended receiver with the fewest errors. The idea of signal space, like the idea of the signal itself and the method of sending it, is basic to today's complex communication systems.

16.
Binary Digits—Cargoes of Information

Now that we've met the zero-one language, let's get better acquainted with its possibilities by looking at a systematic method for assigning meanings and symbols to the o's and 1's of digital signals. Probably you've played a game called Twenty Questions. Someone chooses an item—perhaps an animal or a city—and you have to guess what it is by asking no more than twenty questions that he must answer truthfully with "yes" or "no." If you discover what his item is, you win. If it takes you more than twenty questions, he wins.

Let's suppose your friend has thought of something he thinks will be very hard for you to guess; so he gives you a hint. "The thing I am thinking of is in the dictionary on my desk," he says. That doesn't seem like much of a hint, but you begin anyway.

"Is it an animal?" you ask.

"Yes," he says. You're off to a good start.

"Is it furry?"

"Yes."

"Is it smaller than a camel?"

"Yes."

"Is it a dog?"

"No."

"A cat?"

"No."

You go through a list of other animals, but with no success. Your friend reminds you that you have only three questions left. It occurs to you that maybe it's an imaginary animal. "Is it a unicorn?" you ask.

"No."

"Well, is it a real animal?"

"Yes."

You have only one question left; so you make a blind guess. "Is it a zebra?"

"No, but you're close. It's a zyzzyva."

"A *what?*" you exclaim.

"A zyzzyva. A small weevil that lives in tropical America," your friend says smugly.

"That's not fair," you protest. "I've never heard of a zyzzyva. And besides, you said it was like a zebra."

"I didn't say it was *like* a zebra. I said it was close," he says. "Zebra and zyzzyva are both under Z near the end of my dictionary. In fact, zyzzyva is the very last word in my dictionary."

Is there any way you could have guessed that your friend was thinking of a zyzzyva—even if you had never heard of one? Well, suppose you used a simple plan. First you ask your friend, "Is the thing you are thinking of in the last half of the dictionary?"

"Yes," he says.

"Is it in the last half of the last half?"

"Yes."

"Is it in the first half of the last half of the last half?"

"No."

Now you know it is in the last half of the last half of the last half. You can see as you follow this procedure that your questions are going to get cumbersome very soon; so let's simplify the process. You ask your friend each time, "In the part of the dictionary that is left"—the part you know contains the thing he is thinking of—"is it in the last half?" Every time he says "Yes," you write down a "1." And every time he says, "No," you write down a "0."

After four such questions, your series of numbers looks like this: 1 1 1 1, which means that the word *zyzzyva* was always in the last half of the part of the dictionary that was left after the previous question. How many questions would you have to ask before you know he's thinking of a zyzzyva?

Let's suppose there are 65,536 words in your friend's dictionary. After your first question, you know the word you are seeking is in the last half, or last 32,768 words. After your second question, you know the word is in the last half of the last half, or the last 16,384 words in the dictionary. If you keep asking your question in this way, after fifteen questions you will discover that you are down to the last two words in the dictionary. You ask the sixteenth question. "Is the word you are thinking of the last word of the two that are left?"

He says, "Yes," and you have won with four questions to spare, and without ever having heard of a zyzzyva.

As you may have realized by now, any word in our 65,536-word dictionary can be represented by a string of 16 1's and 0's. For example, the word "A," which is the first word in the dictionary, is represented by 0 0 0 0 0 0 0 0 0 0 0 0 0 0 0, since it is always in the first half of the part of the dictionary that is left. And the 32,768th word—the word just before the middle of the dictionary—is represented by 0 1 1 1 1 1 1 1 1 1 1 1 1 1 1 1 because it is in the first half of the dictionary but is always in the last half of the part that is left.

You may think this is a fine scheme for winning at Twenty Qeustions, but is it good for anything else? Definitely, yes. The whole language of modern communication and computer systems is based on just two words: yes and no, or symbolically in numbers, "1" and "0."

We have seen how strings of 1's and 0's can describe the

location of a word in the dictionary. In a similar way, we can identify each letter in the alphabet with a string of 1's and 0's. In this case we need strings of just 5 digits, since we have only 26 letters to deal with, and not the 65,536 entries in our dictionary, which required 16 digits. In fact, if you figure it out you will see that 5 digits is enough to identify 32 items—more than enough for each letter of the alphabet. Four digits is not enough, however, since 4 can identify only 16 items.

After we have identified each letter of the alphabet with its corresponding string of five 1's and 0's, we can write out any *word* in the dictionary as a longer string of 1's and 0's— or *binary digits,* as they are called because there are just two of them; they are called *bits* for short. We'll hear more about bits in Chapter 17.

We can even write the numbers 0 through 9 as strings of bits. There are many ways this could be done, using not more than 4 bits per number. The table below shows how it is usually done:

NUMBER	REPRESENTATION IN BITS
0	0000
1	0001
2	0010
3	0011
4	0100
5	0101
6	0110
7	0111
8	1000
9	1001

What do we gain by taking a number like 9, just one digit, and turning it into four digits—1001? Well, as we know now, we can express the location of a word in a dictionary as a string of bits; we can express the alphabet and numbers o through 9 as strings of bits. In other words, almost any location in a dictionary or table, or any set of symbols—letters, numbers, or whatever—can be expressed as strings of bits. It's as though we have found a universal language containing just two words—o and 1; and in this very simple language we can express any other language or set of numbers. This is a huge advantage for communication systems and computers because it means that if all symbols can be translated into bits, then the computers and communication systems have to "learn" or manipulate only one language—the "o-1" language.

There are other advantages in the o-1 language. We discussed one of them in the previous chapter. You may recall that the helicopter we mentioned there could receive a wrong message if there was a transmission error—a o changed to a 1, or vice versa. We saw that we could minimize confusion between important messages by placing them at opposite corners of our "cube"—that is, by separating them by great distances in our signal space. If we convert numbers and the letters of the alphabet into strings of binary digits, we expand the volume of our signal space. In this larger volume we can separate the numbers and letters by large distances, so that there is little chance of confusion among them.

Mathematicians and communication engineers have greatly elaborated on the use of signal space. They know how to *code* numbers and letters into strings of bits that will tell whether an error has occurred during transmission; these are called "error detecting codes." There are also "error correcting codes" that not only reveal that an error has occurred, but tell what the error was.

Many messages which we want to transmit are not in the form of symbols such as letters or numbers. For example, as you know by now, when you speak into a telephone the telephone produces a signal that "follows" your voice. When your voice is high pitched, the signal has a high frequency; and when it is low pitched, the signal has a low frequency. When your voice is loud, the signal is strong; and when your voice is soft, the signal is weak. Figure 1 shows a voice signal that changes from weak and high pitched to loud and low pitched.

Let's see how we can turn the signal produced by our telephone into binary digits, and what advantages may result. Figure 2 shows that our signal varies in strength from about 42 to 128. We begin by dividing the signal into a number of equally spaced samples, as shown in the figure. Each sample represents the strength of the signal at the instant the sample was taken. We have now changed our continuous—or *analog* signal, as it is called—into a long series of numbers whose values range from 42 to 128. From the figure we see that the first three samples are 63, 48, and 42.

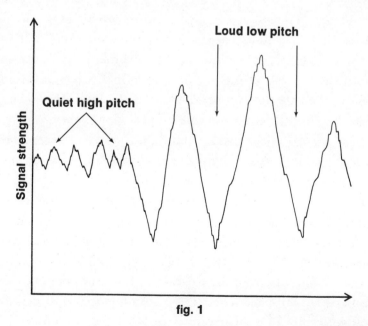

fig. 1

Voice signal from telephone

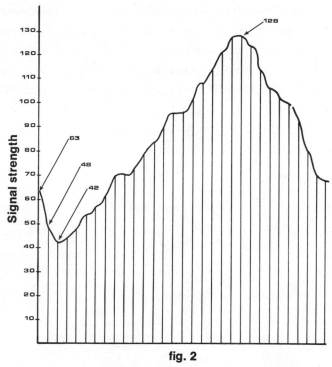

fig. 2

Converting an analog signal to a digital signal

As we've now learned to do, we divide the possible strengths of the signals—0 through 128—into two equal groups. Then we divide these into two groups, and so on, assigning 1's and 0's as we go along. Although we won't do it here, we can show that all the signal strengths, 0 through 128, can be represented by just 7 binary digits. For example, the strength 71 is represented by 1001001.

Now how do we actually transmit the digits? One way is to use the dot-and-dash system used in telegraphy. We simply let a dot stand for 0 and a dash stand for 1, so that a digital telegraph signal would consist of a long string of dots and dashes. This is not the usual method, however, for a reason we shall see in a moment. The usual method is to send a *pulse* of signal when we want to send a 1, and to send nothing when we want to send a 0. In this system, the digital message 1100101 would look like the signal shown in Figure 3-a.

This figure brings out another advantage of digital signals for counteracting noise. The detector in a digital radio receiver has to "decide" only whether a pulse of energy is present or not. If a pulse is present, a 1 has been sent; if not, a 0. In the presence of noise, our digital signal might look like the one shown in Figure 3-b. It's pretty easy to tell where the pulses are, even when noise is present.

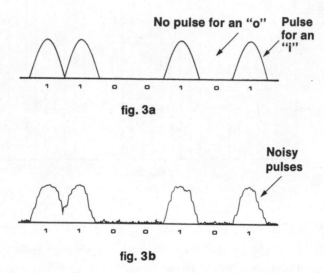

fig. 3a

fig. 3b

If we wished, we could take this noisy signal and put it into a device called a *regenerative repeater,* which "outputs" a new string of noise-free pulses that look like the original pulses in Figure 3-a. Figure 4 shows a regenerative repeater in operation. A typical application is in a long cable carrying digital pulses. As the pulses travel through the cable, they become distorted and noisy. But if a regenerative repeater is placed in the cable every few kilometers, the pulses are continually "cleaned up" so that when they reach the other end of the cable, no matter how long it is, they are practically noise free.

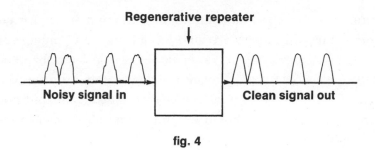

fig. 4

Let's contrast this idea with that of sending a continuous signal, such as an AM or FM signal, through the same length of cable. As with the digital transmission, the signal weakens and becomes noisy. To overcome this difficulty, we place in the cable, every few kilometers, an *amplifier*—built perhaps with triode tubes—to amplify the weakening signal. But this system amplifies the noise as much as it does the signal, so that what comes out at the receiving end is a strong but noisy signal. So we see that *discrete, discontinuous* digital signals can be transmitted with almost perfect fidelity, something that's impossible with AM and FM signals.

Now let's briefly review the steps we have gone through to produce a digital signal. First we started with a continuous signal, like the voice signal shown in Figure 1. Then we sampled it to produce a set of numbers whose values vary according to the strength of the sampled signal. Then we converted these numbers into binary digits, and finally we transformed the digits into pulses for 1's and "no pulses" for 0's. As we might suspect, this whole process is just another form of modulation, like AM and FM, which converts the original signal to some other form that may be broadcast. This kind of modulation is called *pulse code modulation,* or PCM for short.

Any kind of continuous or "analog" signal, such as a radio or television signal, can be relayed using PCM. Today almost all radio and television signals are analog, but in the future we can expect more and more of them to be converted into strings of 1's and o's. We know some of the advantages of this conversion now; but as we shall learn in later chapters, this conversion lays the groundwork for communication systems like the digital TV system we mentioned in Chapter 14, which until recently existed only in the minds of science fiction writers.

17.
Information, Noise, &
Dr. Shannon

We have noted that many of the communication inventions of the nineteenth century were made with little or no understanding of the basic laws that govern electricity and magnetism. In a similar way, many of the schemes for modulating radio signals were developed before there was any really adequate "theory of communication." Armstrong had surprised the experts with his invention of almost static-free FM radio. Obviously, the interaction of signal strength, noise, and bandwidth was more complicated than anyone suspected.

Among the people who began to think deeply about this problem was an American mathematician, Dr. Claude E. Shannon. In 1948, he published a now famous scientific paper titled "A Mathematical Theory of Communication." Shannon was not thinking about a particular communication system such as TV or AM radio; he was interested in developing a theory that would apply to *any* communication system, whether it was an existing system or some system not yet thought of.

Shannon realized that all communication systems have several elements in common. Three of these we have already considered: the strength of the signal, the amount of noise that contaminates the signal, and the bandwidth occupied by the signal.

Everyone agreed that the chances of getting a message through from sender to receiver improved as the signal strength increased—assuming, of course, that the noise did not increase correspondingly. Or if it was not possible to increase signal strength, perhaps means could be found to decrease the noise. In any case, what was important was the ratio of signal strength or power to noise power, a ratio which we shall abbreviate as s/n. What was not yet agreed upon was the effect of signal bandwidth, which we shall abbreviate as B.

Using the idea of signal space, Shannon was able to show that increasing the s/n ratio does improve the chances of getting a message through, and so does increasing B. The surprise was that increasing B helps more than increasing s/n.

Shannon also showed that for a fixed s/n and B, there is only so much information that even a *perfect* communication system could carry. His equations did not give any clue as to how this perfect system could be built, but they did show what the limit would be if anyone was clever enough to build it.

Shannon also realized that another communication system element, in addition to the three we have mentioned, is *redundancy*. Redundancy refers to any part of a message that is repeated. Suppose, for example, that you leave a message for a friend: "I will meet you at noon. I will meet you at noon." This message is redundant because it repeats itself. Efficient communication systems do not provide us with information we already know.

But suppose that instead of leaving a written message for your friend, you were trying to give him the same message over a noisy telephone line. You realize he is having difficulty hearing you; so you repeat the message several times. Finally he understands. In any real communication system some redundancy is always necessary because no system is ever without noise.

In our discussions we have used the words *information, communication, signal,* and *message* rather interchangeably. Shannon knew that before he could develop a communication theory, it was necessary to be more precise in the use of these words. So he decided to define a unit of information which he called a *bit*. Bits are to information what kilometers are to distance. We can talk about 10 bits of information just as we can talk about 10 km.

Exactly what is one "bit" of information? Well, suppose you flip a coin. When it comes up heads, you write down a 1; and when it comes up tails, you write down a 0. After a few flips you might have generated a series of digits that look like this: 110101100100. Each of the 0's and 1's in this string of numbers represents one *bit* of information; since the string is 12 digits long, it represents 12 bits of information. A bit, then, is the amount of information that specifies which of two equally likely events has occurred. When we flip a coin, a head or a tail is equally likely.

As you may have realized, the 0's and 1's making up the digital signals described in the previous chapter are simply bits of information. Furthermore, since any continuous—or *analog*—signal can be converted into a digital signal, we see that any signal, digital or continuous, can have its information content measured in bits. Bits are pieces of information that apply to any communication system; so we can readily compare one system with another by comparing the rate at which each can deliver bits of information.

Let's consider a general communication system that has all the components of any typical system, such as AM radio. Such a system is shown in Figure 1. First we see a box labeled "message source." This box represents someone speaking into

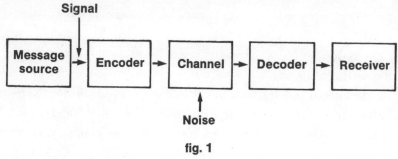

fig. 1

Components of any typical communication system

a microphone, or perhaps a signal from a TV camera. The figure shows the signal that represents the message entering another box called an *encoder*. Encoder is the name applied to any kind of device that changes the message signal into the signal to be relayed. So the output of the encoder could be an AM, FM, or PCM signal.

Next the signal travels through the channel. The channel might be a cable or perhaps the atmosphere. Finally the encoded signal reaches its destination, where it enters the *decoder,* which restores the signal to the form it had when it left the message source.

After the signal leaves the decoder, it enters the receiver. Again, if the signal represents current fluctuations caused by someone speaking, the receiver is simply a loudspeaker or an earphone. Since no channel is ever perfect, the figure also shows noise entering the channel.

Let's suppose now that the message we wish to send over this system is the information we generated by flipping a coin: 110101100100. If we use PCM, the signals leaving the encoder are simply pulses when the message source indicates a "head," and no pulse—or a *space,* as it is usually called—when there is a tail. The bits of information—the pulses and spaces—must leave the encoder at a uniform rate as shown in Figure 2. If this were not the case, it would be difficult or impossible to know how many bits a vacant space between

pulses represented, or alternatively, how many bits a continuous "on" signal represented.

As the signal travels through the channel, it becomes
somewhat distorted because of noise. If the noise is too great,
we may have to add redundancy by repeating messages. Finally the signal reaches the decoder, where the pulses and
spaces are converted back into 1's and o's—bits. The bits enter the receiver, which might be a box with two lights labeled "heads" and "tails." As the lights go on and off, they
indicate the sequence of 1's and o's generated by the message
source.

Suppose now that the person at the message source is

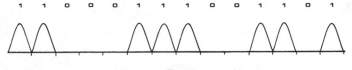

fig. 2

The pulses and spaces must leave the encoder at a
uniform rate

flipping a coin at the rate of one flip per second. This means
that the channel must carry information at the rate of one
bit per second. If the flipping rate is 10 flips per second, the
channel must have a "10-bit per second channel capacity."

As we said, Shannon showed that even for a perfect system there is a maximum channel capacity, which is determined by s/n and B. Let's suppose that the maximum channel capacity of our system is 9 bits per second and we are
flipping a coin 10 times per second. What can we do?

This question leads to another important component in
communication systems—*memory*. Suppose the encoder has
a "memory device" that can remember the binary digits flowing from the message source at 10 bits per second. As the incoming bits pile up in the memory device, the encoder sends

them out of memory at the channel capacity rate—9 bits per second. During one second, 10 bits are stored in memory and 9 are sent out, leaving one bit in memory. For every second of transmission, the memory must store one bit of information; so after 10 seconds of transmission, there are 10 bits stored in memory.

We can see that if the encoder has a maximum memory of 100 bits, then after 100 seconds of transmission the memory will be full and we must stop the message source; otherwise bits of information will be lost, since there is now no place to store them.

Suppose now we replace the coin with a six-sided cube. Five of the sides are marked with a 1, and the sixth is marked with a 0. If we rolled this cube a great many times, we would expect, on the average, to obtain one 0 for every five 1's. In other words, the chances of obtaining a 1 are much better than the chances of obtaining a 0. If we roll the cube once per second, what channel capacity is necessary to let someone at the receiver know which face of the cube has turned up after each roll?

Let's agree to send a pulse whenever a 1 turns up, and a space when a 0 turns up. The message might look something like this after 12 rolls: 011111010111. We notice a big difference between this message and the one generated by tossing a coin; there we had, on the average, as many 1's as 0's, whereas now we have more 1's than 0's. Of course we can expect this, since the chances of obtaining a head or a tail are 50-50, whereas with our cube the chances of rolling a 1 are much greater than for rolling a 0.

What impact does this difference have on the required channel capacity? At first it might seem that there is none. We are rolling the cube once per second to generate a 1 or a 0; so isn't the required channel capacity 1 bit per second?

Well, let's recall the definition of a bit: A bit specifies the result of two *equally likely* possibilities, such as the result of flipping a coin. But with our special cube, the chances of a 1 or a 0 are not "equally likely" at all. A 1 is much more likely. In other words, if you were at the receiver end guessing whether a 1 or a 0 would turn up next, you would be wise to guess 1. When the message is generated by flipping a coin, one guess is as good as the other; the receiver would be just as surprised with a 0 as with a 1. But with the cube, the receiver is more surprised when a 0 turns up than when a 1 does.

This means that the message generated by rolling a cube once per second does not contain as much information as one generated by flipping a coin once per second. Somehow it must be possible to *code* the message so that it requires less than one bit per second.

The key to this coding is to notice that we have strings of 1's with an occasional 0. Suppose we introduce a new code that is 3 bits long. As we know from our helicopter example back in Chapter 15, such a 3-bit code can represent *8* messages, which we mapped onto the corners of a cube. So now we'll use the 8 possible messages to indicate the number of 1's in our message between any pair of 0's, as shown in the following table:

CODE	NO. OF 1'S BETWEEN ANY PAIR OF 0'S
000	0
001	1
010	2
011	3
100	4
101	5
110	6
111	7

With this scheme, our original message, 011111010111, becomes 101001010. This means there are five 1's between the first and second o's, just one 1 between the second and third o's, and two 1's between the third and fourth o's. This message is 9 bits long—three shorter than the original message. This means that our original 12-bit message did not contain more than 9 bits of "actual" information. In fact, we can show by Shannon's theory that the actual information content of the 12-bit message is slightly under 8 bits; but the coding scheme we are using is not the best possible, so we had to use 9 bits.

With a 1-bit-per-second channel capacity, it would take 12 seconds to send the 12-bit message. But with coding, the same message takes only 9 seconds. That is, every 12-second message is collapsed into a 9-second message; the average bit rate is 9/12, or 0.75 bits per second. Since our channel has a 1-bit-per-second capacity, we have a 0.25 bit-per-second capacity to spare. We've assumed that the channel is noise-free, however; so we might need this spare capacity to add a little message redundancy to overcome the noise.

Most of today's communication systems are not very efficient. They are not coded to remove unnecessary information, and information we already know is sent over and over. Television is a good example. When we watch the news, we see the newscaster's changing facial expressions and gestures. The map behind him and the desk in front of him, however, do not change. If the TV set had "memory," we would not need to send again and again the part of the signal that "paints" the map and desk. We could code TV signals to contain only the new information—that is, only what is changing in the picture.

A number of systems now being developed—including digital TV—use memory and coding to gain efficiency. Now that we know something about Shannon's Theory of Communication, we're in a better position to understand and appreciate these systems.

18.
Transistors by the Thousands

The idea of pulse code modulation was developed in the 1930s, and engineers and scientists quickly realized its advantages. By using PCM and regenerative repeaters, it would be possible to send almost error-free signals over great distances. But there was no practical way to build equipment to generate, distribute, receive, and store PCM signals.

Using PCM for an ordinary telephone conversation, for example, would require sending more than 50,000 bits of information per second. At a lower bit rate, the quality of the voice signal would be lower than what we're used to with common analog telephone signals. So to gain the advantages of PCM, we must have a great deal of equipment that is much more complex than that used to handle analog signals.

First we need equipment to change the analog signals into digital signals. Then we need special channels that can carry many thousands of bits of information per second. At the receiver end we need equipment to convert the digital signals back to analog signals. And if we wish to remove redundancies in the digital signals, we need more special equipment at both the transmission and reception ends.

The practical problems that had to be solved to make PCM a reality seemed insurmountable. And then in 1948, the same year that Shannon presented his "Mathematical Theory of Communication," a short news item appeared in the July 1 issue of *The New York Times*. Just eight sentences long, it began, "A device called a transistor, which has several applications in radio where a (radio) vacuum tube ordinarily is employed, was demonstrated for the first time yesterday at Bell Telephone Laboratories."

The inventors of the transistor—John Bardeen, William Shockley, and Walter Brattain—received the Nobel prize in physics in 1956 for their invention that revolutionized the whole science of electronics, including telecommunication. Their work shows clearly the enormous changes in scientific investigation between Bell's invention of the telephone in 1876 and their invention of the transistor in 1948. Whereas Bell had almost stumbled into his invention because he could not understand German very well, Bardeen, Shockley, and Brattain deliberately set out to develop an entirely new kind of device that would take the place of vacuum tubes in a variety of electronic circuits, including the amplifier and oscillator circuits we have discussed.

Their search centered on substances like silicon and germanium, which can be turned into *semiconductors*. As the name suggests, a semiconductor is a substance midway between good conductors like copper and good insulators like glass. The idea that devices made from semiconductor materials could be made to operate like diode and triode tubes is based on a set of laws that govern the interactions of atoms with each other and with electrons. These laws were developed over a period of time, starting shortly after Rutherford's discovery that the atom consists of a compact nucleus surrounded by swarms of electrons.

Different kinds of atoms have different numbers of electrons that circle around their nuclei. For example, only one

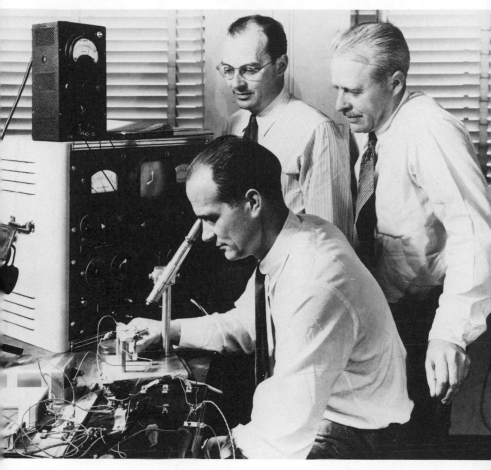

Shockley, Bardeen, and Brattain (l. to r.)
received a Nobel Prize
for inventing the transistor.

electron circles the nucleus of the hydrogen atom, and two
circle the helium nucleus, as shown in Figure 1.

Just as the planets circling the sun are not all at the
same distance from the sun, electron orbits are also at different distances from the nucleus of an atom. In the helium
atom, for example, its two electrons circle the nucleus in the
same size orbits or *shell,* whereas in the silicon atom, with 14

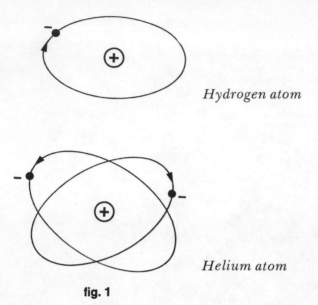

Hydrogen atom

Helium atom

fig. 1

electrons, the first two circle the nucleus at the same distance from the nucleus, the next 8 at a somewhat greater distance, and the remaining 4 at an even greater distance, as shown in Figure 2.

If we looked at the arrangement of electrons around a great many different kinds of atoms, we would notice that the shells containing the electrons fill up in a very systematic

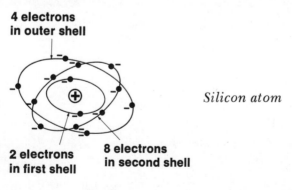

4 electrons in outer shell

Silicon atom

2 electrons in first shell

8 electrons in second shell

fig. 2

way. Each shell has a fixed capacity, and when it becomes full, electrons start filling the next outer shell. The first shell is full when it contains 2 electrons, the second when it contains 8, and the third also when it contains 8. Since the silicon atom has only 4 electrons in its third shell, there is room for 4 more electrons there.

Atoms tend to arrange themselves so that the outer shell is filled as nearly as possible to its maximum capacity. In a crystal of silicon, for example, the atoms are arranged symmetrically so that by "sharing" electrons, the outer shell of each atom contains a full 8 electrons. Figure 3 shows 4 silicon atoms sharing electrons to fill each other's shell. Since all of the electrons in this arrangement are needed to fill, by sharing, the outer shell of each atom, silicon is a poor electrical conductor; there are no "spare" electrons to make up an electric current.

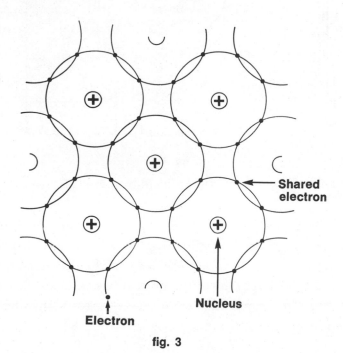

fig. 3

Four silicon atoms sharing electrons

Suppose now we replace one of the silicon atoms with an atom that has 5 electrons in its outer shell. Phosphorus is such an atom. Now 4 of the 5 electrons can be shared as before to complete the shells of adjacent atoms, but the fifth electron is "spare"; so it is a "free" or "conduction" electron, as shown in Figure 4. Thus, replacing a few of the silicon atoms with phosphorus atoms turns a poor conductor like silicon into a semiconductor.

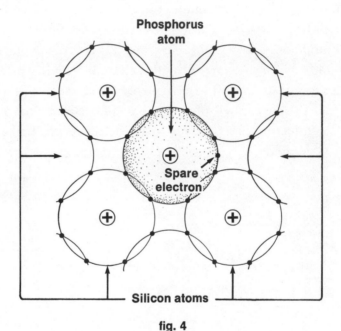

fig. 4

A phosphorus atom supplies one "spare" electron

This replacement process suggests another possibility. Suppose that instead of replacing silicon atoms with phosphorus atoms, which have 5 electrons in the outer shell, we replace the silicon atoms with boron atoms, which have only 3 electrons in the outer shell. Now one electron is missing, as shown in Figure 5, at the point labeled "x." Such a missing electron is called a *hole*.

Although it may seem strange, holes can conduct elec-

tricity; they represent places where electrons are missing, and
this amounts to the same thing as a positive charge. We can
visualize holes conducting electricity by imagining a group
of people sitting side by side on a long bench. Except for the
person at the left end, all wear identical red hats. The woman
second from the left removes her hat and places it on the
head of her hatless neighbor. Then the man next to her removes his hat and places it on her now hatless head, and so

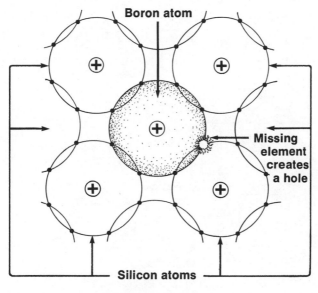

fig. 5

A missing electron leaves a "hole"

on down the line. If this process took place very rapidly, it
would appear that a hatless person was moving from left to
right, whereas in reality all that is happening is a shifting of
hats. The shifting illustrates the flow of electrons, and the
apparent hatless person moving to the right illustrates conduction by a hole.

Thus moving *holes* represent conduction of *positive*
charge, and moving *electrons* represent conduction of *nega-*

tive charge. The process of replacing atoms in silicon with other kinds of atoms is called *doping*. If silicon is doped with a substance like phosphorus, it is called an *n-type* semiconductor because it contains negative conduction charges represented by excess electrons. If the silicon is doped with boron, it is called a *p-type* semiconductor because it contains positive conduction charges represented by the excess of positively charged holes.

Suppose now we take a small chunk of each type semiconductor and join them as shown in Figure 6-a. If we connect the "p-end" to the positive terminal of a battery and the "n-end" to the negative terminal, the excess electrons

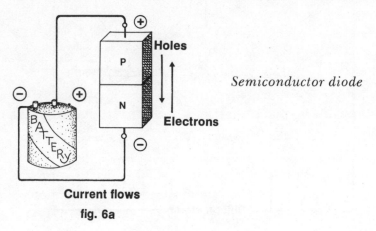

Semiconductor diode

Current flows

fig. 6a

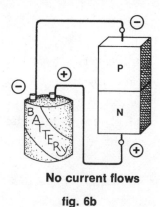

No current flows

fig. 6b

from the n-type semiconductor will flow toward the positive terminal; and the excess holes from the p-type semiconductor will flow toward the negative terminal. But if we reverse the terminals, as in Figure 6-b, no current will flow because the holes will be repelled by the positive terminal and the electrons will be repelled by the negative terminal. In other words, current will flow only one way in this device—which is identical to the operation of the diode vacuum tube we learned about earlier. So now we have created a *semi-conductor diode* that can transform alternating current into direct current just as a diode vacuum tube performed the same task.

Now suppose we take two chunks of n-type semiconductor and a very thin chunk of p-type semiconductor and join them as shown in Figure 7. We now have a *transistor.* The end of the transistor connected to the positive terminal of the battery is called the *collector,* and the end connected to the negative terminal is called the *emitter.* The thin slice of p-type semiconductor in the middle is called the *base.*

These three parts of the transistor are similar to the three parts of a triode tube. The emitter is like the filament, since it is made from n-type semi-conductor; it has excess electrons that it can emit, just as the filament in the tube boils away electrons. The collector serves the same function as the plate in the triode, since it collects the electrons flowing from the emitter. The base plays the part of the grid, since by changing the charge on the base it is possible to regulate the flow of current between the collector and the emitter.

Figure 7 shows just how the transistor operates. First, using a low voltage battery, we put a slight positive charge on the base, which attracts the excess electrons from the emitter. Some of the holes in the base are also attracted toward the emitter, since its charge is negative. So we have a charge flowing between emitter and base. If we compare the

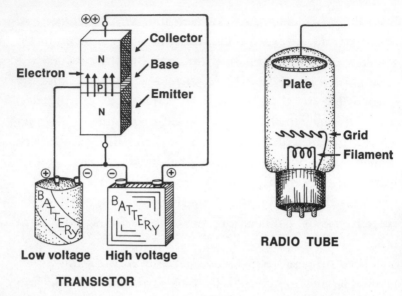

TRANSISTOR

RADIO TUBE

fig. 7

"emitter-base" part of the transistor with Figure 6-a, we see that this part looks just like a diode with the correct charges on the emitter and base to allow current to flow.

What happens to the electrons flowing from the emitter? It might seem that they would enter the base and then flow along the base toward the positive terminal of the battery connected to the base. But as the figure shows, most of the electrons flow across the base into the collector. The reason is that the base is extremely thin; so before the electrons can "turn the corner" to flow along the base to the positive terminal of the battery connected to the base, they have already crossed into the collector; here they are strongly attracted to the positive terminal of a high-voltage battery connected to the collector. Just as slight variations of charge on the grid of a triode tube cause large changes in current flow, so slight changes in charge of the base of the transistor cause large changes in the flow of current between emitter and collector. In this way the transistor acts as an amplifier.

The first transistors were a little larger than a match-head. But advances in their construction have made it possible to pack thousands of transistors on an area no larger than your little fingernail. These highly concentrated aggregates of transistors are the *chips* we first mentioned in Chapter 2. A recent chip less than 2 millimeters on a side contains almost the entire circuitry of an FM radio; only the tuner, speaker, and antenna are outside the chip. Compact-

This tiny chip
can perform
a million operations
per second.

ness is not the only advantage of chips, however; they practically never wear out, they consume very little electrical power, and they are very cheap.

The transistor was the answer to the enormous amount of circuitry needed to handle the thousands of bits of information generated and transmitted by PCM communication. Some circuits make certain that the bits flow along the proper paths. Others generate bits from analog signals or turn digital signals back into analog signals. And still others store bits until the bits are needed. The simplest "storage" circuit requires at least one transistor to store one bit of information; so it takes thousands of transistors to store just one second of voice conversation in digital form. You can see now why practical PCM was impossible with tubes. If we replaced every transistor in a PCM system with a tube, the space needed for the tubes would occupy whole buildings, the cost would be astronomical, and parts of the system would melt from the heat generated by the mass of tubes.

In addition to making PCM possible, the transistor has replaced most of the tubes in practically every electronic device. We have transistor radios and transistorized TV sets. Our tape recorders and stereo systems are built with transistors, and so are the ignition systems of some of the newest model cars. As we shall see, present-day satellites would not be possible without chips, since the cost of launching massive satellites jammed with tubes would be enormous. The satellite would consume very large amounts of power, and it would probably fail after a short time.

19.
Transmitters in the Sky

"An 'artificial satellite' at the correct distance from the earth would make one revolution every 24 hours; that is, it would remain stationary above the same spot and would be within optical range of nearly half the world's surface. Three repeater stations, 120 degrees apart in the correct orbit, would give television and micro-wave coverage to the entire planet." So wrote science fiction writer Arthur C. Clarke in 1945.

Today hundreds of satellites surround the earth, and more than 70 of them are solely for communication purposes. But in 1945 Clarke's vision seemed preposterous to many—something for science fiction only. No satellite of any kind had ever been put into orbit, and no one knew what the earth's atmosphere would do to radio signals traveling back and forth between the earth and a satellite. To launch the satellite Clarke had in mind—one that would stay at the same spot in the sky—would require a rocket powerful enough to put a fairly large satellite in orbit nearly 36,000 km above the earth's surface.

Thirteen years later, in 1957, Russian scientists launched their first *Sputnik*. It was about the size of a basketball and was only a few hundred kilometers above the earth at its highest point. In the early days of Sputnik, however, most people were not concerned about its height or what usefulness it might have. The fact that it was up there at all was puzzle enough. What kept it up? Why didn't it fall back to earth?

The answer is that it did fall continuously toward the earth in its circular journey. But the earth, being curved, fell away under the Sputnik at just the right rate to maintain a constant height between earth and satellite, as shown in Figure 1. First we see the satellite at point A moving in its circular journey toward B. If it did not fall toward the earth, it would continue in the straight-line path shown by the broken line. Because of its circular path, it falls a distance by the time it reaches B; but because of the earth's curvature, the satellite is the same height above the earth at B as it was at A.

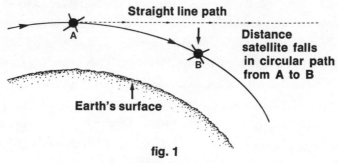

fig. 1

Sputnik fell constantly toward the earth

The time it takes a satellite to circle the earth depends on its height above the earth. A satellite at 300 km takes about 90 minutes, and one at 1,000 km takes about 100 minutes. The higher the satellite, the longer it takes to make one complete orbit. A satellite 36,000 km above the earth takes 24 hours for a complete orbit. Since it takes the earth 24 hours to make one complete revolution, if this satellite happens to be situated above the earth's equator it appears to stand still at one spot in the sky.

Satellites of this kind are called *synchronous* satellites

because their motion is synchronized with the motion of the earth. Today most communication satellites are synchronous, but the first were not because the early rockets were not powerful enough to lift them to the required height.

Clarke used the phrase "repeater station." He meant that the satellite would have on board a radio receiver that would receive a signal transmitted from earth and a transmitter that would relay the received signal back to earth. In today's satellites this receiver-transmitter combination is called a *transponder*. But the first communication satellite did not work this way. Scientists were not sure how electronic equipment would survive in space. What would cosmic rays and the frigid environment do to a transponder's delicate electronic circuitry? No one knew, and no one wanted to take a chance.

In 1960 the United States launched a satellite called "Echo I." It was simply a spherical plastic balloon about ten stories high covered with a thin layer of aluminum. The whole balloon weighed about 60 kilograms, and it was placed in an orbit about 1,600 km high. In a sense the balloon was nothing more than what we might call a "small chunk of artificial ionosphere" because it did nothing but reflect signals from its shiny aluminum surface back to earth. Although the balloon worked quite well, it eventually lost its shape. Tiny meteors punctured its thin skin, letting out the inflating gas.

The first successful satellite containing a transponder was launched in 1962. Called "Telstar," it relayed the first color TV signals across the Atlantic Ocean. Several other communication satellites followed Telstar, but the first successful commercial satellite, named "Early Bird," was launched in 1963. It was in a synchronous orbit and could relay 240 two-way telephone conversations between two earth stations at the same time.

Many improved versions of Early Bird have been sent

*Telstar was the first
communication satellite
to relay TV signals
across the Atlantic Ocean.*

into orbit, and today a single communication satellite can handle thousands of telephone circuits, color TV broadcasts, and even data generated by computers—all at the same time. A single satellite can also interconnect a large number of ground stations, perhaps oceans apart. Satellites today handle about two-thirds of all international communications, involving over a hundred countries and more than 200 ground stations. This enormous communication capability of satellites results from two things: First, rockets are available to launch heavy satellites; and second, the satellites can contain an incredible amount of circuitry because of the invention of chips.

How is it possible to keep this mass of information flow from getting all tangled up? How does each message reach its correct destination, and how does a single satellite relay signals from many ground stations to many other ground stations all at the same time?

Let's take the last question first. The two main schemes that allow a single satellite to handle information from a number of ground stations are called *Frequency Division Multiplexing,* usually called FDM, and *Time Division Multiplexing,* usually called TDM. These are big words for something that is really rather simple. In fact, you are already familiar with FDM, although we did not call it that. You may recall that in AM radio each station is assigned a particular *carrier frequency*—the frequency you tune the dial to to get a particular station—and that the bandwidth of 10 kHz is given to each carrier frequency.

One station, for example, may be assigned a carrier frequency of 850 kHz; so including the 10 kHz bandwidth, the actual signal could occupy frequencies ranging from 845 kHz to 855 kHz. Another station might be assigned a carrier frequency of 870 kHz; so it occupies frequencies ranging from 865 kHz to 875 kHz. In this way the total band of frequencies reserved for AM radio can be split up into a number of channels—one for each radio station. This is an example of FDM, and the bandwidth of a transponder can be split up in a similar way.

On one of today's typical communication satellites, the transponder bandwidth is 36 million Hz, or 36 megahertz (MHz). It takes about 3,000 Hz (3 kHz) of bandwidth to convey a telephone conversation with reasonable fidelity, but let's use a 4 kHz bandwidth just to be on the safe side. Since our transponder bandwidth is 36 MHz, we can split it up into 9,000 telephone channels: 36 MHz divided by 4 kHz equals 9,000.

One band of frequencies for transmission to a satellite ranges from 5.925 billion Hz, or gigahertz, to 6.425 GHz. So our particular transponder might operate in frequencies ranging from 5.925 GHz to 5.925 GHz plus 36 MHz or 5.961 GHz.

Thus, as shown in Figure 2, telephone conversation Number 1 is transmitted to the satellite on a channel 4 kHz wide centered on a carrier frequency of 5.925 GHz plus 2 kHz, or 5.925002 GHz. Conversation Number 2 is on a 4 kHz-wide channel centered at 5.925006 GHz, and so on, ending with conversation Number 9,000 centered on a carrier frequency of 5.960998 GHz.

The transponder on the satellite does not transmit the signals back to earth over the same set of channels, but uses a new set with frequencies ranging from 3.7 GHz to 3.7 plus 36 million Hz, or 3.736 GHz, as shown in the figure. This helps to avoid confusion. After the 9,000 conversations are returned to their ground station, they are processed and routed into the normal telephone system, where each reaches its designated telephone.

In our example we transmitted information to the satellite at frequencies near 6 GHz and back to earth at frequencies near 3.7 GHz. Future satellites will use even higher frequencies. Earlier satellites, however, used much lower

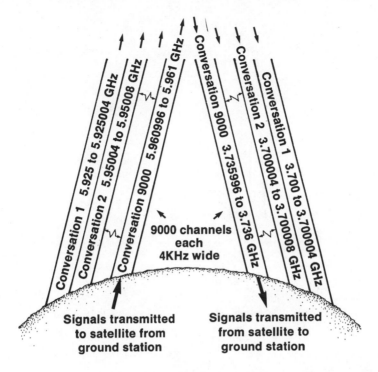

Conversation 1 5.925 to 5.925004 GHz
Conversation 2 5.95004 to 5.95008 GHz
Conversation 9000 5.960996 to 5.961 GHz
Conversation 9000 3.735996 to 3.736 GHz
Conversation 2 3.700004 to 3.700008 GHz
Conversation 1 3.700 to 3.700004 GHz

9000 channels
each
4KHz wide

Signals transmitted
to satellite from
ground station

Signals transmitted
from satellite to
ground station

fig. 2

Frequency Division Multiplexing

frequencies—as low as 20 MHz. At these low frequencies, the
ionosphere can distort a signal, and in some cases even reflect
the satellite signal back out into space.

In FDM, we divided the transponder bandwidth into a
number of channels, with each channel assigned a share of
the total bandwidth. In TDM, we divide the transponder into *time* "chunks" instead of frequency portions. Figure 3
shows how this system works. Four ground stations—A, B, C,
and D—are transmitting information to the same satellite.
The information from ground station A is shown in three
boxes labeled B, C, and D. Information in Box B is for
ground station B; information in Box C is for ground station C, and so on. The boxes from the other three ground
stations have similar destinations.

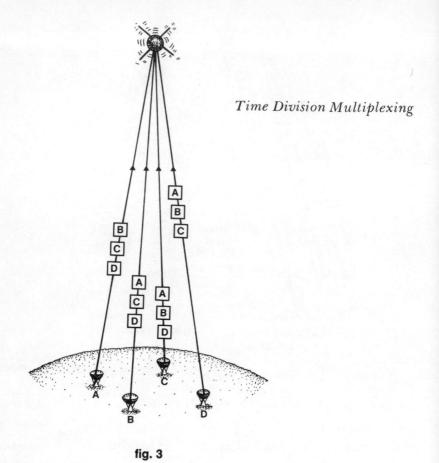

fig. 3

Let's suppose now that the information contained in Box B from ground station A arrives at the satellite first. The transponder rebroadcasts this information back to earth, where it can be received by all four ground stations. This is shown in Figure 4 by the elongated Box B that is nearest to the earth.

Suppose now that Box C from ground station A reaches the satellite next. This information is returned to the earth as shown by elongated Box C, which arrives just after Box A from ground station A. In a similar way, each of the boxes of information is sent in turn from each of the ground stations,

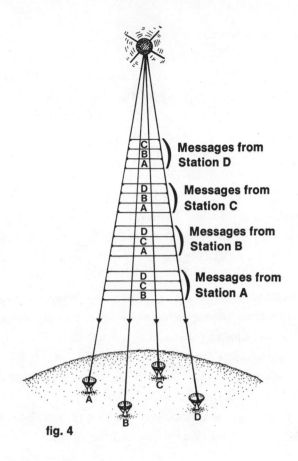

Messages from Station D

Messages from Station C

Messages from Station B

Messages from Station A

fig. 4

and each is returned to the earth in the same sequence. The messages from ground station D are last.

Although each of the ground stations receives all of the messages, a particular ground station can select out only the messages intended for it by knowing the *timing* sequence of the various messages from the four stations. In other words, each ground station must know ahead of time which will transmit what messages in what order. Timing—sometimes to a millionth of a second—is very important in TDM because if a particular station transmits at the wrong time, two packets of information may arrive at the same instant and cause the satellite to retransmit a confused jumble of information. Very precisely synchronized clocks are a vital part of the system.

Most of today's communication satellites use FDM because the equipment is simpler than for TDM and there is not the time problem. A few of the latest communication satellites use TDM, however; and in the future probably all communication satellites will use TDM because it is a natural way to relay signals that are pulse code modulated.

Let's consider a particular example that shows how PCM and TDM go hand in hand. Suppose we wish to relay three telephone conversations from point A to point B via a satellite, as shown in Figure 5. The three telephone signals arrive from the callers at ground station A, as shown by the arrows marked 1, 2, and 3. In TDM we have to divide the signals into time packages, or *time slots* as they are usually called. This is done by a rotating switch that first "samples" the strength of conversation 1, then 2, then 3, then 1 again. If the switch rotates very rapidly, the samples of signals will resemble the original signal very accurately.

This process is identical to the one we discussed in Chapter 16, where we demonstrated how a continuous analog signal can be turned into a series of numbers whose values indicate the signal strength at the time the signal is sampled. In this case, however, the rotating sampling switch produces *three* discontinuous signals.

The next step is to convert the numbers representing the signal strengths into strings of pulses and spaces—that is, to turn the sampled signal strengths into PCM. This process occurs in the box labeled "modulator" in the figure. The signals leaving the modulator are strings of pulses and spaces, which are sent in turn, as shown. The first signal arriving at the satellite is a group of pulses and spaces representing a sample of conversation Number 1; the second group represents Number 2, the third Number 3. Then the pattern repeats.

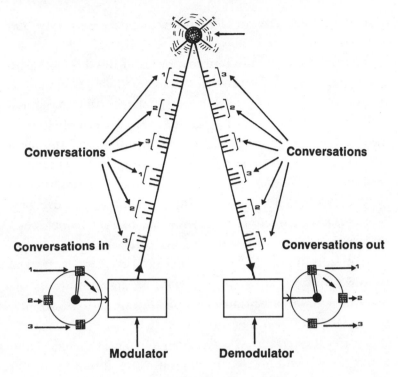

Conversations

Conversations

Conversations in

Conversations out

1

2

3

1

2

3

Modulator

Demodulator

fig. 5

TDM and PCM work well together

The satellite relays these digital signals back to ground station B in the order received, as the figure shows. Here a device called a *demodulator* turns the PCM signals back into the numbers representing the sampled signal strengths. These are then fed to another rotating switch that separates and feeds the signals into the telephone lines labeled 1, 2, and 3.

The rotating switches at A and B must stay exactly in step; otherwise conversation Number 1 from A may be sent out on line Number 2 from B, or perhaps pieces of all three conversations from A will be sent out on all three lines from B. In some communication satellites using TDM, the bit rates may be more than one million per second. Without today's extremely precise clocks, such timing would be impossible.

Before we conclude our discussion of satellites relaying digital signals we should mention one other advantage of PCM. As we know by now, any signal can be transformed into PCM—phone calls, TV signals, data generated by computers, music, any kind of signal we can think of. This means that all signals can be transformed to a standard type, independent of what they represent. So we don't need different kinds of equipment to handle different kinds of signals. Once they are transformed to PCM, all signals can be processed the same way and sent down the same channels.

In spite of the fact that communication satellites can transmit millions of bits of information per second, the demands for communication are growing so rapidly that eventually satellites won't be able to handle all of the desired communication traffic. In the next chapter we shall learn about a new kind of system that can carry billions and billions of bits of information per second.

20.
Talking Through Glass

The telegraph replaced the semaphore in the late 18th century, and it is only in the last few years that scientists have again given serious thought to the idea of using light signals for sending messages. Yet much of what we already know about radio communication applies to communicating with light—or *optical* communication, as it is usually called.

First we need some source of information—someone speaking into a microphone, for example. Then we need some way to impress this information on a light beam, or to "modulate the carrier," as we expressed it in discussing radio. The carrier, however, is not a radio wave, but a light wave. Next we need some channel to carry the light signal. It could be simply a beam of light passing through the atmosphere, or the light signal might be guided in a tiny strand of glass as fine as a human hair.

At the receiving end we need some device to detect the light signal, and in this particular case, some device to convert the modulated light signal back into the sounds of the speaker's voice.

So far, optical communication sounds almost the same as communicating with radio waves. But there is one dramatic difference: The bandwidth we can obtain with optical signals is 10 million times larger than is possible with radio waves.

We know that the communication capacity of a system increases as its bandwidth increases. But the bandwidth is limited by the carrier frequency. Since the bandwidth occupies frequencies from the carrier frequency plus the bandwidth to the carrier frequency minus the bandwidth, the bandwidth can never be greater than two times the carrier frequency. For example, a system with a 1 MHz carrier frequency could have a total bandwidth of 2 MHz—1 MHz plus 1 MHz to 1 MHz minus 1 MHz. If we try to increase the bandwidth to more than two times the carrier frequency, we come up with less than 0 MHz at the lower limit—an impossibility, since we can't have negative frequencies.

With this limitation in mind, let's compare the communication capacity of a 100-MHz signal—which happens to be in the FM band—with the communication capacity of an optical signal. To make our comparison a little easier, we'll assume that the bandwidth of a system can always be at least 10 percent of its carrier frequency; so the bandwidth of our 100-MHz system is 10 MHz. The frequency of a light wave can be as high as 1 billion MHz; so 10 percent of this frequency gives us a bandwidth of 100 million MHz. That is, the bandwidth of the light wave signal is 10 million times greater than that of the 100-MHz signal. Or stated differently, the communication capacity of the optical system is 10 million times greater than that of the radio system—assuming that both systems have bandwidths that are the same percentage of their respective carrier frequencies.

Let's try to put this enormous communication capacity of optical systems into terms we can comprehend. Typically each frequency in the bundle of frequencies making up the bandwidth allows us to transmit one bit of information per second; so if the bandwidth of our optical system is 100 million MHz, we can send 100 million million bits of information per second.

Suppose now that we have a huge library filled with nothing but books 500 pages long—not very likely, but it makes the arithmetic easier. How much information from this library could we send in one second?

Well, a book 500 pages long contains roughly 5 million bits of information; so our optical system could transmit an astounding 20 million "books' worth" of information in one second! This is about the number of books in the Library of Congress, in Washington, D.C.

This example illustrates what is possible in principle. It assumes that we have devices that can modulate a light beam fast enough to produce 100 million million bits of information per second. No such device exists today, but there are devices that have allowed scientists, on an experimental basis, to transmit the equivalent of 40,000 books per second.

You may recall that one of the big problems with the Hertz transmitter was that it generated signals that "splashed" over a whole band of frequencies, and that what was needed was a transmitter that would generate just one frequency. As we have seen, such a single-frequency transmitter could be modulated to carry information.

One of the reasons that optical communication was so slow to get started was that no one had been able to build a "light transmitter" that generated just one frequency. The light from a light bulb or a fluorescent tube is a jumble of many different frequencies. But in the spring of 1960, a single-frequency light source was developed by an American scientist, Dr. Theodore H. Maiman. These devices are called *lasers,* and they are used for everything from drilling tiny holes in metal to surgically "welding" a torn retina in the human eye.

To understand the operation of a laser, we must go back

to our model of the atom with its compact nucleus and circling electrons. You'll recall that electrons circle the nucleus in well-defined orbits. An electron can jump from one orbit to another, and it is this movement of electrons between orbits that generates light.

To see how this works, let's consider nature's simplest atom, the hydrogen atom. Figure 1 shows the hydrogen atom with its one electron circling the nucleus. The orbit labeled "1" is the closest possible orbit to the nucleus, and other, farther-out possible orbits are labeled 2, 3, 4, and so on.

Suppose two hydrogen atoms collide. The collision may be enough to knock the electron from orbit 1 into orbit 4. Just as it takes energy to climb from the first floor of a building to the fourth floor, it takes energy for an electron to go from the first to the fourth orbit. Here, however, the electron is "climbing" against the electrical force between the nucleus and the electron, not against the earth's gravitational force. This energy is provided by the two atoms when they

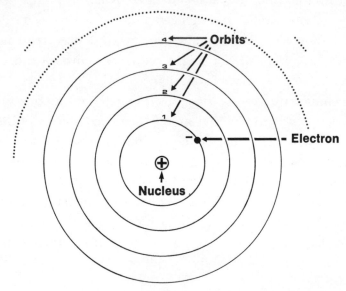

fig. 1
Hydrogen atom

collide; so the total energy of the atoms resulting from their motion is a little less after the collision than it was before. This loss of "energy of motion" is just the required amount to kick the electron from the first to the fourth orbit. Other collisions might kick the electron into other orbits—the second or third, perhaps.

The natural state of a hydrogen atom is to have its electron in the lowest or number 1 orbit. So eventually the electron will spontaneously jump from 4 back to 1, although it may make intermediate stops on the way, as shown in Figure 2.

When an electron jumps to a lower orbit, what happens to the energy that it gained when it moved to a higher orbit? Somehow the atom has to give up that energy when the electron jumps to a lower orbit. This is how light is generated. When the electron jumps from, say the fourth to the second

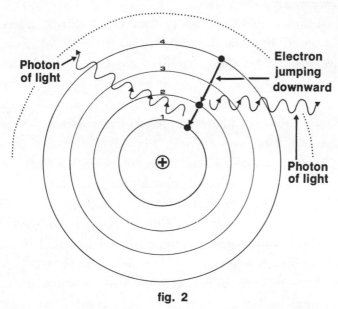

fig. 2

Every time an electron drops to a lower orbit, a photon of light is produced

orbit, the atom emits a small packet of light energy called a *photon*.

Let's apply this idea to the operation of a fluorescent tube, which is filled with mercury vapor. By turning on the switch connected to a fluorescent tube, we cause a stream of electrons to flow through the tube, some of them slamming into mercury atoms and knocking electrons into higher orbits. As the electrons return helter skelter to lower orbits, the atoms emit radiation in a random, disorganized way in different directions; the radiation strikes a "fluorescent" material coating the inside of the tube, creating the familiar light.

Suppose now that we could force all of the electrons to jump to lower orbits in an *organized* rather than a disorganized way, so that the light waves were all "in tune," so to speak, moving all in one direction with crests and troughs representing their frequency in alignment. If we could do that, we would have a laser.

Although there are many different kinds of lasers today, we shall describe the first one built by Dr. Maiman because it illustrates rather simply how light at a single frequency—or *coherent* light, as it is called—can be produced. The heart of Dr. Maiman's laser was a small rod made of synthetic ruby, about the diameter of a pencil and about 9 centimeters long, as shown in Figure 3. The two parallel ends of the rod were polished and coated with silver, to provide a mirror effect. Coiled around the ruby rod was a flash lamp that could create an extremely strong flash of light. When the lamp flashed, some of its photons collided with some of the ruby atoms, kicking electrons into higher orbits.

The trick now was to get the "elevated" electrons in the ruby atoms to jump downward in an organized way to produce coherent light. As we said, the elevated electrons in atoms normally jump down spontaneously in random fashion; but there is a way they can be *made* to jump down.

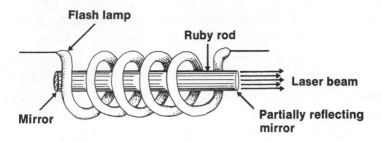

Flash lamp

Ruby rod

Laser beam

Mirror

Partially reflecting
mirror

fig. 3
Ruby laser

Suppose a photon generated by one of the ruby atoms
with an elevated electron comes in contact with another ruby
atom with an elevated electron. This causes the electron in
the second atom to jump down, producing a photon at exactly the same frequency. We now have two photons traveling together in step. These two photons may contact two
other excited atoms, so that now we have four photons in
step. Figure 4 shows how the process keeps building up so
that eventually we have many photons, all in step, producing
coherent light.

Some of these photons reflect from the mirrors on either
end of the tube and are directed back into the rod, while

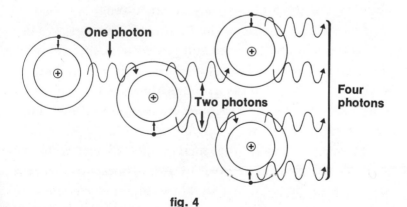

One photon

Two photons

Four
photons

fig. 4

The chain reaction of released photons produces a laser

others traveling in other directions escape from the rod. The photons reflected back into the rod cause other atoms with elevated electrons, which have been missed thus far, to radiate. So as the photons keep bouncing back and forth between the two mirrors, more and more photons, all in step, are created.

If one of the mirrors is only partially reflecting, a small amount of light will escape with all the crests and troughs in step, producing coherent light. Now we have a laser.

Although we shall not go into the details here, a number of methods have been developed to modulate laser beams to produce continuous-type signals—perhaps with amplitude modulation or frequency modulation—or to produce streams of pulses. As we said, the carrying capacity of laser beams today is limited by the speed with which the modulation can be carried out. In a way, we're back to the old problem of the semaphore, where the message itself traveled at the speed of light, but the awkwardness of the ropes and pulleys and the need to repeat everything before relaying it made the system slow.

Although a modulated laser beam can be sent through the atmosphere, transmission distances are limited because of dust particles, rain drops, clouds, and other "contaminants" in the air. And laser beams sent through the air cannot penetrate walls or go around corners. Most laser signals are channeled through hair-thin strands of glass. The number of pulses per second that can be sent through a glass fiber depends on the fiber's construction. Although there are many considerations, we'll discuss just one very basic one here—the diameter of the fiber.

Strangely enough, the smaller the diameter of the fiber, the more pulses it can channel per second. Figure 5 shows why. Fiber A is a glass filament about 100 one-millionths of a meter in diameter; below it is the smaller fiber B, with a diameter of about 5 one-millionths of a meter. The

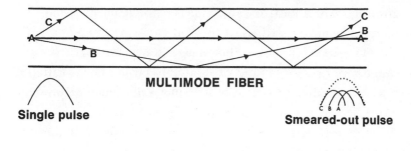

MULTIMODE FIBER

Single pulse

Smeared-out pulse

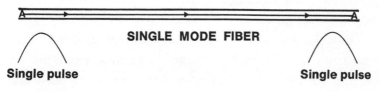

SINGLE MODE FIBER

Single pulse

Single pulse

fig. 5

The smaller the glass fiber, the more pulses it can carry per second

rays marked a, b, and c in the larger fiber show possible paths the pulses might take through it. The inside surface of the fiber acts like a mirror; so a pulse may pass straight through the fiber, or it may bounce back and forth. The shortest path, a, is down the center of the fiber; so a pulse taking this path arrives at the end of the fiber first. But part of the energy of the pulse may take other, longer paths, such as b and c; path c is longer than path b because it makes more zigzags.

The part of the pulse's energy that takes these longer paths arrives at the end of the fiber later than the energy that took path a. So what started out as one large narrow pulse at the beginning of the fiber ends up as three smaller overlapping pulses at the end of the fiber, as shown. Together they produce a "smeared out" pulse, indicated by the broken line. This smearing out limits the pulse capacity of the cable, since the pulses at the transmission end must not be so close together that what is really two or three pulses at the beginning may appear as just one smeared-out pulse at the receiving end of the fiber.

These various paths the energy in a pulse may take are called *modes;* so this kind of relatively large fiber is called a *multimode* fiber. If the fiber's diameter is sufficiently small, like fiber B in the figure, only one mode is possible—right through the center of the fiber. There is no problem with overlapping, and the distance between pulses at the end of the cable is just the same as it was at the beginning.

Optical communication is relatively new, and many improvements must be made. Two of the greatest needs are for better devices to detect the pulses at the receiving end, and for other devices to handle the enormous amount of information that optical systems can communicate. In spite of these and other limitations, however, many systems are already in operation and others are planned. At Walt Disney World, in Orlando, Florida, optical fibers carry a variety of information such as voice, music, and data to regulate and monitor the many exhibits. One of the most ambitious projects is in the planning stage. The Bell Telephone Co. plans to construct a 1,000-km optical system between Washington, D.C., and Boston, Massachusetts, that will handle 40,000 telephone conversations at once. In the next chapter we shall see the need for optical communication systems to handle the information requirements of tomorrow's systems.

21.
2001: A Communication Odyssey

What will communication be like in the first part of the 21st century? Making forecasts is risky. Many experts underestimated the rate at which satellites would be introduced for communication, and they predicted videotape recorders for home use decades before they were available. For years we've been hearing about the picture phone, but we still don't have it. Sometimes eminent scientists and engineers—usually committees of them—are asked to advise presidents and other heads of state on the probable success of some project. All too often they say that something can't be done—and this seems to be just enough incentive to inspire others to prove that it *can* be done.

When Thomas Edison announced his invention of the electric light, the British parliament set up a committee of experts to investigate his claims. Their conclusion was that his ideas might be "good enough for our transatlantic friends, but they are unworthy of the attention of practical scientific men." So much for the predictions of experts.

Though we don't know much about tomorrow's communication systems, we can probably be more definite about the "blocks" from which future systems will be built, whatever their "shape." Certainly one of the blocks will be high-speed equipment like that used in the optical system we have just explored. Another block will be the integrated circuit, or chip, in which thousands of circuit elements are jammed onto an area no larger than a pinhead. Even today whole computers are so small that four of them can be laid end to end inside the perimeter of a paper clip. Communication satellites will also continue to be important building blocks. And most messages—telephone, television, data—will probably be built from streams of on-off pulses—PCM, for example.

From this handful of building blocks we can construct an enormous variety of communication systems with incredible complexity. In a sense the real problem is more *What shall we build?* than *How shall we do it?* Time, financial backing, trained personnel, laboratory facilities, and other resources are limited. New needs for safety in aircraft operation or for defense against some new weapon developed by another nation demand new communication capabilities and methods. Often it's hard to sort out worthwhile projects from the frivolous. Some new invention may make something feasible that was prohibitively expensive before. The general economy, and even politics, enter into decisions on communication systems. But in spite of these uncertainties and the fact that we are not experts, let's plunge ahead with our predictions.

One of the keys to tomorrow's communication systems will be flexibility. We can see a hint of this today by looking at what is happening to TV sets. You have doubtless seen, and perhaps have in your own home, a device that can be attached to a TV set so that you can play games on it. The screen of a TV set can become a football field or a race track, and you can control the movement of players or the motions of cars with a small, hand-held "control box" that communicates your instructions to the TV set.

Many people today also have video tape recorders, so

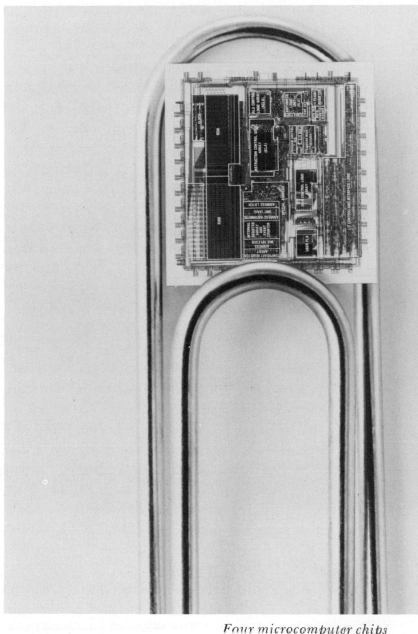

*Four microcomputer chips
like this one
can fit inside
the perimeter of
a standard paperclip.*

that they can record whole TV programs for later viewing, or perhaps buy prerecorded video cassettes of favorite movies, which they can view on their home TV sets.

Other changes in TV may be less familiar to you. You may have noticed that the TV log in your newspaper lists some programs as "closed-captioned for the hearing impaired." This means that a person who cannot hear the TV broadcast can *read* what is being said during the program if he has a TV set that includes a special chip. The captions appear at the bottom of the screen in much the same way that foreign movies are subtitled.

The captioning system is in some ways quite different from ordinary TV, and it includes some of the features that future communication systems will use. First, the captions are sent as digital signals, whereas ordinary TV signals are of the continuous or analog type. Second, the captioning system is very efficient, since once a caption is sent it is not repeated. This is very different from ordinary TV, in which the same picture is sent over and over, 30 times a second, even though it does not change. As we said earlier, the same picture has to be sent repeatedly because the TV set has no "memory," and once the picture transmission has ended, the picture disappears from the screen. A captioning TV set has special electronic circuits that can "remember" a caption once it has been sent, and the caption remains on the screen until a new caption is sent. So the captioning system uses digital signals, and memory to avoid redundant messages— two of the important components in advanced communication systems.

How are the digital signals sent so that they don't interfere with the regular TV signals? We have learned that the movement in a TV picture, as in a movie, results from showing a series of slightly different "still" pictures—30 pictures per second, which is rapid enough to give the illusion of continuous motion. But between every two still pictures

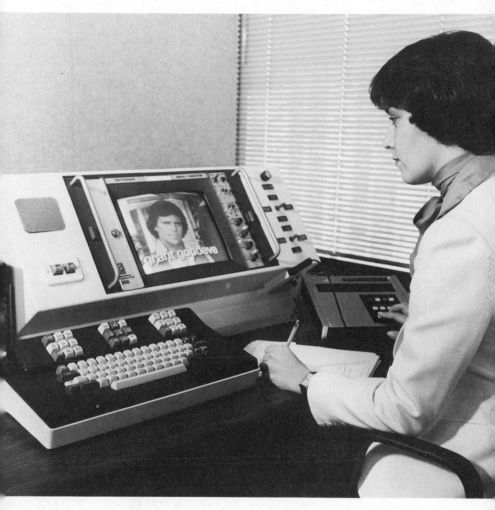

This editor is
preparing captions
for the hearing impaired,
which can be seen
on special TV sets.

there is a very short interval when no picture is broadcast. The digital signal for captions is sent during that interval. A special chip in the TV set "extracts" this short burst of digital signal, decodes it, and displays it as words at the bottom of the TV screen.

In this captioning system, the information is "sandwiched" into ordinary TV signals. Other kinds of information such as stock market reports, local weather information, emergency messages—anything that can be expressed in words and numbers—can be sent in this same way. Today this kind of expanded information capacity of TV is called "teletext," a system we mentioned in Chapter 3.

Other systems use telephone lines to carry information for display on TV sets. Figure 1 shows the main components of such a system in England called "Prestel." A user with special equipment can dial a certain telephone number and ask for a particular piece of information—a recipe for making chocolate fudge, perhaps. The recipe, stored in the memory of a computer, is sent back to the user, as a digital signal, over a telephone line. The signal is decoded and displayed on the user's home TV set.

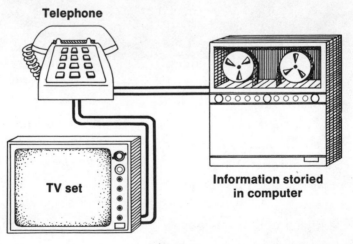

Telephone

TV set

**Information storied
in computer**

fig. 1

Prestel

This system is an example of how TV and the telephone can be "married" to offer new kinds of services that each system alone cannot provide, and such a marriage points to two other important features of tomorrow's communication system: First, the viewer gets the information when he wants it. He doesn't have to wait until 8:00 on Thursday evening when the "chocolate fudge" program is playing. And second, unlike ordinary TV, in which the viewer simply receives what the station sends, this system is "two-way."

The telephone, of course, is a two-way system, since we can use it for both speaking and listening. But the telephone has a serious limitation; the amount of information it can handle is very small. The bandwidth of ordinary telephone channels is only about 3 or 4 kHz, whereas a thousand times that much is needed for TV signals. So although a telephone channel is sufficient to carry very limited information, such as a recipe that appears on the screen as words, it cannot handle large quantities of information that need to be sent in a very short time.

A few cities in the United States and the rest of the world are experimenting with what is called two-way cable TV. The telephone lines are replaced by special cables that can carry large amounts of information from the user to the TV station and from the TV station to the user. With this system the viewer can request that the TV station send a particular program whenever he wants to see it. Or perhaps the viewer wants information on how to repair his particular make of automobile. This kind of information can be stored in the memory of a computer at the TV station. In fact, four of today's large computers have enough memory to store all of the information contained in the Library of Congress.

Other implications of two-way cable TV could have a profound effect on society. With two-way cable TV as common in our homes as our present one-way sets, governments could get, almost instantly, public opinion on a particular situation. Issues could be debated on TV, and viewers could respond immediately as to which point of view they supported.

We could have electronic newspapers that would give us information tailored to our own interests. Suppose, for example, that you wished to buy a used ten-speed bicycle. You might have a particular brand and price range in mind. If you live in a large city, you would probably want to try to find a bike that is not too far from where you live. In other words, you have a certain set of qualifications that define your particular need, and you are not interested in reading a large number of classified ads for bikes of no interest to you.

With what is today called a "smart" TV set, you could see only the ads that meet your specifications. A smart TV set is simply one that contains a computer, which because computers are so small today, can easily be placed inside a regular TV cabinet. You tell the computer, perhaps using a typewriter-like keyboard, the particular type of bike you are looking for, and the computer sorts through the electronic classified ads and sends your TV set the signals to display only the ones that meet your needs.

Smart TV sets offer more possibilities. Computers can be given different sets of instructions—or *programmed*—to perform different tasks. The computer in your TV set could be programmed with a keyboard, or the program could be electronically transmitted to your TV set from some other location.

Suppose, for example, that you wished to play the newest kind of video TV game, which all your friends are talking about—an electronic version of "Kingdom," perhaps. With two-way cable TV, you could instruct the computer at the TV station to send the program required to play this game to the computer in your TV set.

The game may require two or more players. So you arrange for several of your friends to request that the same program be entered into their smart TV sets, and you also request that the TV sets in your friends' homes—which may be in different parts of the city, or even in different cities—all be connected so that you all see the same "game board" and each other's moves.

The game may take several hours, and you and your friends may not have time to finish at one sitting. So you agree to continue tomorrow at 4:00 P.M. Now you instruct the computers in your TV sets to remember each player's position so that you can start tomorrow at the point where you left off. Or you could instruct the computer at the TV station to remember the state of the game at the stopping point.

Of course we are a number of years away from such advanced electronic game playing, and the hundreds of possible commercial uses for a system with these capabilities are far more important than mere entertainment. But the example we've used is well within the capability of the handful of building blocks we already have. The computers and the necessary memory circuits are built from chips. The signals, representing a wide variety of information, program instructions, moves of players, the game board, and even voice communication among you and your friends are all in digital form.

There are two big advantages of digital signals that we have not yet mentioned. First, most computers are what are called *digital* computers. That is, their "natural" language is based on the on-off pulses we are now familiar with. If our signals are already in digital form, they can be handled directly by computers, we don't have to translate them into some other language so that the computer can "understand" them. Second, the order of the on-off pulses can easily be "scrambled" at the transmitting end and "unscrambled" at the receiving end, to protect the privacy of a message.

If you imagine millions of people all playing electronic games or sorting through electronic ads at the same time—or performing any one of a hundred other possible activities you can think of—you begin to see why we will someday need the enormous communication capacities of optical fibers. All the telephone lines, copper cables and satellites that connect the world in today's communication web could not possibly serve the needs. The cost of stringing new copper cables to meet these needs—assuming there is even enough copper in the world to build them—would be astronomical. And strange as it may seem, there is not enough room out in space for all the satellites required for such vast amounts of communication.

These facts bring us back to the limitations of time and resources that keep us from realizing all of the many possibilities. But in a way, the handful of building blocks that create all the possibilities also point to a solution to the problems. There is so much flexibility in the communication systems of tomorrow that each user can have a system tailored to his own needs. Not everyone needs or wants every possibility. Today the "candy store" of communications is pretty much limited to the telephone, radio, and television. But from tomorrow's communication candy store you will be able to choose from many varieties, and take a little or a lot.

We are already used to this kind of approach in a limited way. Many high-fidelity audio systems are put together from components. You may buy a certain kind of speakers from one store, the turntable from another, and your choice of amplifiers from a third. Similarly, you may buy the components of tomorrow's home communication system from different stores, and perhaps add new components to it from time to time. Different people will have different components in their systems.

As an example, you may wish to see the evening news

displayed on your TV screen, and you may also want a permanent record of some particular news item. So you will need some device to print out the news on paper, or to provide what is called "hard copy." Your neighbor may not care about hard copy, so he doesn't need that device. But he may wish to subscribe to a burglar alarm service that protects his home electronically; if a stranger enters his home while he's at work, the police are notified immediately, electronically. Figure 2 shows an example of possible compo-

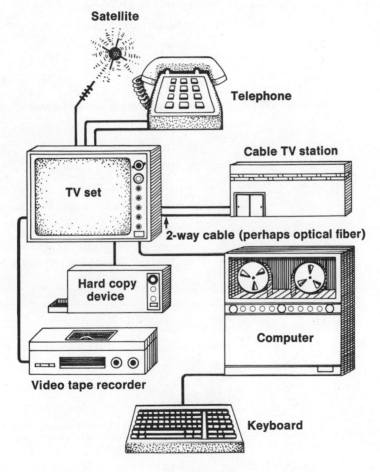

fig. 2

Tomorrow's home communication center

nents in tomorrow's home "communication center."

We have come a long way since Øersted's dim suspicion that electricity and magnetism were connected, and since Maxwell's theoretical prediction that radio waves existed. Yet what we have today is just a beginning to what many scientists say is a "transition from the industrial age to the communication and information age." In our final chapter we shall explore what some scientists and philosophers see as the greatest communication adventure of all time, and others have called an utter waste of time, talent, and money.

22.
Listening to the Stars

If we could board a rocket ship and move away from the earth at the speed of light for the next few hundred thousand years, we would see—if we looked back over our shoulder—a vast, spiraling empire of stars. At the center of the spiral we would see a bright, luminous bulge teeming with millions of stars and thinning out toward the edge. This spiraling disk of stars, thick at the center and thin at the edges, is our own galaxy, the Milky Way, the home of our nearest star, the sun, which is one of about 100 billion stars in our galaxy.

If we looked ahead two million more years of travel into the distance, we would see another spiraling array of stars, the Andromeda galaxy, an almost identical twin to our own. When we look at Andromeda through a powerful telescope, we are close to knowing how we appear to someone studying us from a distant planet.

Is there someone out there studying us? Or are we alone in this almost endless universe of stars—a universe of at least 10,000 billion billion stars? This question has intrigued mankind for thousands of years. Although the question is old, it is only in the last 20 years that we have had the tools to pursue the answer.

The Andromeda Nebula
is much like
our own
Milky Way Galaxy.

But knowing that we have the tools does not mean that the search will be short or easy. There are seas of stars to inspect for intelligent life whose probable means of signaling and communication we can only guess at. Some scientists have said that the chances for success are so small that the search is not worth the effort, and is in fact ridiculous. But others point out that although the odds are microscopic, the implications of success are so great that we cannot afford *not* to look. Success might mean an incredible shortcut to knowledge—knowledge gained by civilizations millions of years ahead of ours.

Besides the possibility of reaping the benefits of thousands or millions of years of labor by intelligent beings in some distant corner of the universe, there are tremendous implications for man's understanding of his own place in the universe. Until about 400 years ago, men believed that our earth was at the center of the universe, with the sun, moon, and stars circling overheard. When Copernicus challenged that notion in 1543, he not only laid one of the foundation stones of modern astronomy, but forced man to reexamine long-held beliefs about his own importance and position in the universe. No doubt the discovery of intelligent life beyond the borders of our planet would once again force us to reexamine our position and our uniqueness in the "universal scheme of things."

In spite of the uncertainty about when, where, how, and perhaps most of all, why to look, some 50 different organizations in several countries have started to sift the stars for signs of intelligent life. They've looked at about a thousand stars to date.

If you had the task of designing such a search, how would you proceed? Exploring the universe with rocket ships seems out. They are too slow, and costs are very high just to reach nearby planets such as Venus or Mars. Radio waves are much faster—as far as we know there is nothing faster—and much cheaper.

By now we know a good deal about radio waves and how to use them for communicating. We know that three of the most important factors are signal—both its strength and its form—noise that contaminates the signal, and bandwidth. We also know that we can both transmit and receive signals, and this brings us to our first decision: Should we talk or listen?

Since we've had the technology to communicate over interstellar distances only for the past two decades, it seems likely that we are infants in the business, and that others know how to generate radio signals far more powerful than our technology allows. So we are probably better off to concentrate on listening.

This brings up the next question: If we are listening, what kind of signal should we expect? This is a very difficult question because we have no idea what form intelligence takes outside our earth. Probably the best we can do is assume that "their" intelligence is something like ours, and imagine that they would do what we would do. It seems reasonable, for example, that they would not send radio signals that would get confused with other "natural" radio signals like the radio noise generated by stars and other material in interstellar space. This kind of noise tends to be random; so we would expect an intelligent signal would not be random, but would be somehow regular and systematic—like someone knocking on the door rather than the door banging aimlessly in the wind.

We would also expect a signal to be transmitted in a part of the radio band that is relatively quiet. As we have said, the stars and interstellar material generate radio noise that can interfere with signals. If we look at this noise, we find that it is relatively quieter in a band of frequencies from about 1,400 MHz to about 1,600 MHz; so it seems reasonable that we should tune to frequencies in this range.

The last factor to consider is bandwidth. As we know, the larger the bandwidth, the more information a radio signal can carry. But that is only one consideration. If the amount of energy a distant transmitter can broadcast is limited—even though it might be very large by our standards—using a large bandwidth means that the energy will be spread over a wide range of frequencies; so the energy at any particular frequency may be very weak.

On the other hand, if the bandwidth is small, the energy will be concentrated in a small bundle of frequencies; so the energy at any particular frequency may be quite large, and the chances of detecting the signal are better because it is stronger. This reasoning assumes, of course, that we happen to tune in to the correct narrow band of frequencies. Although we cannot be sure of the best strategy, the tendency is to assume that the signals will be "narrow band" and therefore strong.

Now we come to the biggest unknown of all: Is there anybody out there to send messages at all? It's safe to say that your guess is as good as anybody's, including the "experts."

There are several ways to attack this problem. One is to try to estimate how many stars are like our own and how many of them might have planets that could support life. The factors that go into this approach are so uncertain that almost any answer is possible.

Another, more "down to earth" approach is simply to ask, If there are lots of intelligent beings out there, where are they? After all, civilizations well advanced beyond our own probably know how to build space ships whose speeds approach the speed of light. And it is not beyond believability that some of these advanced civilizations have colonized the planets of nearby stars. Within 100 light years of our own planet, for example, there are probably at least a thousand stars similar to the sun; one light year is the distance we could travel in one year if we traveled at the speed of light. Although even traveling at the speed of light it would take hundreds of years to explore this relatively small region of our galaxy, this is not necessarily a problem for an advanced civilization that may know how to maintain life almost indefinitely.

In any case, the "Where are they?" argument seems to suggest that the number of advanced intelligent civilizations is not exceedingly large—at least not in our neighborhood. On the other hand, this argument certainly does not prove that there are *no* civilizations out there. So we're back to where we started. Your guess is as good as anybody's.

We've suggested that any kind of intelligence-bearing signal will have some regularity to it. But this brings up another and perhaps more difficult problem. We may be convinced that we have intercepted an intelligent message from space, but what does the message mean? After all, there are some ancient languages here on earth still not decoded, and presumably they were developed by people who had at least some of the same concerns and desires that we have. How could we possibly decode messages developed by beings we know nothing at all about? Perhaps we cannot. We may be convinced that beings are there and sending messages, but we may never know what they are "talking" about.

But this thought may be too pessimistic. It seems reasonable that our galactic neighbors would want to design messages that other intelligent beings would have some hope of decoding. How could they do this? Well, we know that in any kind of communication there must be some common ground of understanding. If *we* wished to communicate with a distant planet, for instance, we would probably not choose to transmit a TV picture of a horse; the chances are too great that there are no creatures on that planet that look like horses. Animals on earth are "shaped" to fit their environment: fish are streamlined to glide through the water, and birds have wings to ride the air. Surely creatures on other planets have evolved to fit their own particular environment, which may be very different from ours. So we must look for some common ground that is more nearly universal and more abstract. We need some feature or development that would be characteristic of *any* intelligent society with the means of interstellar communication.

Two possibilities come to mind—there are probably others. The first is the "laws of physics." It seems likely that the laws of physics are the same at every point in the universe. The speed of light is the same in the farthest galaxy as it is in our own. And the laws that govern the "burning out" of distant stars are the same ones that govern the demise of our own sun. Perhaps we could talk to each other about physics.

The other possibility—and the one we shall consider more fully—is a conversation about mathematics. Presumably $1 + 1 = 2$ and $2 \times 2 = 4$ everywhere in the universe. Let's suppose we received this message from space: $\cdot$ $\cdot\cdot$ $\cdot\cdot\cdot$ $\cdot\cdot\cdot\cdot$. We might imagine that these dots represent the numbers 1 through 4. But this message could also mean a lot of other things. We need more information to confirm our suspicion. We need something to trim down the possibilities.

Suppose the message continued like this: $\cdot$ — — $\cdot$ — $\cdot\cdot$ $\cdot\cdot$ — — $\cdot\cdot$ — $\cdot\cdot\cdot\cdot$. We first guess that $\cdot$ — — $\cdot$ — $\cdot\cdot$ means $1 + 1 = 2$, where — — means $+$ and — means $=$. This seems to make some sense because with this interpretation the message that follows— $\cdot\cdot$ — — $\cdot\cdot$ — $\cdot\cdot\cdot\cdot$ —means $2 + 2 = 4$. But suppose the beings on planet X do their arithmetic backwards, so that we should read the messages from right to left instead of left to right. In that case we could interpret the messages to mean $2 - 1 = 1$ and $4 - 2 = 2$, where the dots still have the same meanings, but where the meanings of $-$ and $- -$ are reversed.

But then come another two messages: $\cdot - - - \cdot \cdot - \cdot \cdot$ and $\cdot \cdot - - - \cdot \cdot - \cdot \cdot \cdot \cdot$. The $- - -$ seems to be a new symbol. Since we suspect that the messages are about arithmetic, let's guess that $- - -$ means "times," for which we usually use the symbol "$\times$." Then the last two messages become $1 \times 2 = 2$, and $2 \times 2 = 4$, if $-$ means $=$.

If we assume the other possibility, that $-$ means $-$, and read the messages backwards, we get a nonsensical result: $1 \times 2 - 2$, $2 \times 2 - 4$. So we conclude that $-$ probably means $=$. This example suggests that if we receive enough examples of how the symbols are used, eventually a particular symbol will be "trapped" into a specific meaning that could have no other interpretation.

Of course, all of this is pure speculation, since no such messages have ever been detected and we are in the embarrassing situation of guessing what someone else might do. But the scheme does suggest a way that civilizations could build up a language if they had some common ground of understanding in the beginning. In a way it's like going clear back to the very beginning of language. Receiving a message from somewhere in outer space that said only $2 + 2 = 4$ would certainly be both the most exciting and the most tantalizing thing that has ever happened to Earthlings. We would want to know at once what these beings are like, how they live, and what else they have to say. But it would take at least 12 years just to let them know that we'd heard their $2 + 2 = 4$, even if we knew how to reply and everything worked right, and the communicators were on a planet circling the star closest to us which is most like our sun.

Even so, as we said, a number of organizations are scanning the skies for some sign of intelligent radio signals. One of the most impressive facilities is the Arecibo Observatory

*The huge dish-shaped antenna at Arecibo, Puerto Rico,
listens for interstellar messages. The Arecibo Observatory
is part of the National Astronomy and Ionosphere Center
operated by Cornell University under contract with the
National Science Foundation.*

in Puerto Rico. Here a huge antenna in the shape of a dish, with an area of nearly 20 acres, has "listened" since 1975 for some faint signal from space.

But huge as this antenna is, many scientists think it is not big enough. Several suggestions have been made, but one in particular has received considerable attention. Called "Project Cyclops," it would consist of an array of perhaps as many as 1,500 antennas, each one a hundred meters in diameter. The antennas would all be connected to each other and to a large computer, to make the equivalent of one enormous antenna with a collecting power many hundreds of times greater than any existing facility. Such an antenna could detect ordinary TV signals from civilizations hundreds of light years away.

Are the possible results from such an enormous project worth the cost? Is it even worth spending time using the facilities we already have? Perhaps our situation is like that of Columbus when he was getting ready to set sail. He thought he was heading for India, but instead he found a new continent. So although we may not be successful in our search for intelligent life beyond our solar system, we would no doubt discover new "continents" while trying.

The gamble is great, but in the words of Guiseppe Cocconi and Philip Morrison, who first proposed in 1959 that we begin to search: "The probability of success is difficult to estimate; but if we never search, the chance of success is zero."

GLOSSARY

For better usefulness and understanding, the words in this glossary are grouped logically instead of listed alphabetically.

Telecommunication—Communication at a distance

Bit—A unit of information that specifies the outcome of two equally likely events

Electron—A basic particle of nature that carries negative electric charge

Electric field—A region of space characterized by the existence of a detectable electric force at every point

Magnetic field—A condition in a region of space characterized by the existence of a detectable magnetic force at every point

Electromagnetic wave—The wave predicted by Maxwell that has both electric and magnetic characteristics

Conductor—A substance such as iron or copper that conducts or carries an electric current

Nonconductor—A substance such as glass that conducts little or no electricity

Signal—A sign, mechanical device, or electric impulse used as a means of communication. Also the message sent or received by such means

Analog signal—A continuous signal, in contrast to one that is broken into discrete "samples" for transmission

Digital signal—An intermittent or discontinuous signal, in contrast to an analog signal

Radiation—The emission and propagation of light, sound, or radio waves

Ionosphere—A region of the earth's upper atmosphere that reflects radio signals

Noise—Any disturbance that interferes with the transmission of information

Frequency—The number of repetitions per second of a complete electromagnetic wave

Carrier frequency—The frequency of the electromagnetic wave that is modulated to convey information

Amplitude modulation (AM)—Conveying information by changing the strength or amplitude of a signal

Frequency modulation (FM)—Conveying information by changing the frequency of the signal

Bandwidth—The range of frequencies occupied by a signal

Hertz (Hz)—A unit of frequency equal to one cycle per second

Kilohertz (kHz)—one thousand cycles per second

Megahertz (MHz)—one million cycles per second

Gigahertz (GHz)—one billion cycles per second

Electrode—A metal disc in a vacuum tube that either emits or collects current

Anode—A positively charged electrode

Cathode—A negatively charged electrode

Plate—The positively charged electrode in a radio vacuum tube

Filament—The heated wire in a radio vacuum tube that emits electrons

Grid—The electrically charged element in a radio vacuum tube that regulates the flow of current between the filament and the plate

Diode—A radio vacuum tube with two elements—a plate and a cathode

Triode—A radio vacuum tube with three elements—a grid, a plate, and a cathode

Transistor—A very tiny electronic device that can take the place of a radio vacuum tube

Chip—An electronic device, sometimes called an integrated circuit, containing many transistors and other circuit elements, compressed into an area no larger than one's little fingernail

Laser—A device that generates light waves at a single frequency

Optical fiber—A hair-thin strand of glass that guides light signals

INDEX